THE CRESCENT, KING STREET
ORDERLY PLANNING OF *c.*1825, TOWARDS THE END OF THE CLASSICAL TRADITION

HISTORY
IN LEICESTER

COLIN D. B. ELLIS
MC, MA, FSA

History in Leicester

55 BC — AD 1976

The Old West Bridge

Information Bureau

Recreational and Cultural Services Department

Bishop Street Leicester

Copyright © 1976
Information Bureau
Recreational and Cultural Services Department
Leicester City Council
Bishop Street
Leicester

SBN 901675 156

First published 1948
Second edition 1969
Third edition 1976

PRINTED BY LEAD, NUTT & STEVENS LTD.
LEICESTER

PREFACE TO THE FIRST EDITION

THOSE of us who have lived our lives in or near Leicester know how much it has changed within our own recollection and within the recollection of people whom we have known. We are able to explain, more or less, what the town was like fifty years ago and how and why it has turned into what it is like to-day.

In writing this little book I have tried to carry the inquiry and the explanation farther back; to find out and explain what the town was like when it was first founded and how it changed and developed until it became what it was when I first remember it. What I have written is not, of course, the whole truth. The most I can claim is that it is as much of the truth as I could find out in a short time and set down in a few words. The most I can hope is that I have put down the more important of the many things that happened and that I have indicated the more important of the many reasons why things happened as they did.

For those readers, I hope the majority, who will accept my narrative only as a *prima facie* case and who wish to form an independent judgment, I have added to the narrative, in each part, a short list of books which they can read for themselves, a short description of buildings which they can see for themselves, and the testimony of a few witnesses, for the most part contemporaries, which they can weigh for themselves.

I should, perhaps, say something about the division of the narrative into periods. This arbitrary arrangement was adopted partly for convenience and partly because both the pace and the direction of Leicester's development did change, sometimes abruptly, at certain times. But it would have been equally logical, if it had been equally convenient, to break the narrative at other points—at the Black Death, or at the Reformation, or at 1836 for example. And wherever the break had been made, except perhaps at the end of the Roman era, and possibly even then, it would be necessary to emphasize that though there was a change there was nevertheless continuity. I cannot do better than quote a paragraph from the introduction to G. M. Trevelyan's *English Social History*.

In political history one King at a time reigns; one Parliament at a time sits. But in social history we find in every period several different kinds of social and economic organization going on simultaneously in the same country, the same shire, the same town. Thus, in the realm of agriculture, we find the open-field strip cultivation of the Anglo-Saxons still extant in the eighteenth century, side by side with ancient enclosed fields of the far older Celtic pattern, and modern enclosures scientifically cultivated by methods approved by Arthur Young. And so it is with the varieties of industrial and commercial organization—the domestic, the craft, the capitalist systems are found side by side down the centuries. In everything the old overlaps the new—in religion, in thought, in family custom. There is never any clear cut; there is no single moment when all Englishmen adopt new ways of life and thought.

So much for my own part in this book: it remains for me to acknowledge the important part in its preparation that has been played by others.

Mr. Kenneth Holmes has supervised the format and Mr. Hugh Collinson has taken entire charge of the illustrations, selecting appropriate prints and photographs for reproduction, drawing the necessary maps and contributing, I am very glad to say, a drawing of his own.

I have discussed my own drafts with a number of people, to whom I am indebted for corrections and suggestions. In particular I should like to mention Mr. Frank Cottrill, Mr. S. H. Skillington, Dr. W. G. Hoskins, Mr. W. Keay, Mr. C. A. Parker, and Mr. A. T. Patterson, who have freely placed their special knowledge at my disposal. They have saved me from many blunders: for those that remain my own obstinacy or carelessness must be held responsible.

I have to thank Lt.-Colonel W. Butler-Bowdon and Messrs. Jonathan Cape for permission to include the valuable extracts from *The Book of Margery Kempe* which are copyright material.

Finally, I must express my gratitude to Alderman C. R. Keene, without whose encouragement I should probably never have written this book and who has been largely responsible for the business side of the publication as well as for bringing it before the Publicity Committee of the Leicester City Council which has approved its issue.

May 1947   C.D.B.E.

PREFACE TO THE SECOND EDITION

THE call for a new edition has enabled me to make various amendments to the text and to incorporate two major changes.

Much exploratory work has been possible during the last few years on the centre of Roman Leicester which has been uncovered by excavations for new roads. I have asked Mr. M. Hebditch, who has taken part in these excavations, to re-write my first sections in the light of his new knowledge.

For me 'history' naturally ended roughly where my personal recollections began and so the first edition of this book finished at the turn of the last century. I accept however that for those younger than myself 'history' can come up to a much more recent date, and I have therefore asked Professor Simmons, who was brought up elsewhere, to add a Part giving a new summary of the town's development since 1900. Professor Simmons is grateful to Dr. J. B. Priestley and Messrs. Heinemann for granting him permission to include extracts from *English Journey*.

Mr. W. R. M. McClelland, the City Librarian and Publicity Officer, has assisted me in preparing this edition for the press and has given especial care to the selection of new illustrations, eight of which are from his own photographs.

C.D.B.E.

June 1969

PREFACE TO THE THIRD EDITION

IT is sad to record that shortly after the publication of the second edition in 1969, Colin Ellis, who had been ill for some time, died. The book has sold steadily over the six years and a new edition has become necessary because stocks are exhausted and, with the passage of time, there are some alterations to be made to the text. The major altera- tions come unexpectedly at the beginning and, predictably, at the end.

Jean E. Mellor, B.A., Field Archaeologist, Leicestershire Museums, Art Galleries & Records Services, has completely re-written the sections on Roman Leicester. This reflects the intensive research that has been carried out during the intervening years on sites made available by the redevelopment of old buildings. Modern history, of course, never stands still and the past few years have seen some very fundamental changes, especially in the structure of local government. Professor Simmons, has, therefore, brought his chapter up-to-date.

Despite local government reorganisation, responsibility for publicity in Leicester has remained with the City Council and the task of preparing this edition has fallen upon the Recreational & Cultural Services department. The Information & Publicity Officer, Margaret Fotheringham, B.A., A.L.A., has been responsible for all the pains- taking work of up-dating the bulk of the text and preparing the book for the press. A number of minor changes have been made in the main part of the text, taking into account changes of street names and opening hours and such developments as the completion of the restoration of Roger Wygston's House and its opening to the public as a Costume Museum. There are several new maps and illustrations and we are grateful to Leicestershire Museums, Art Galleries & Records Services, University of Leicester and the Leicester Theatre Trust for permission to reproduce them.

This work remains a fine memorial to a man who cared a great deal for and gave so much of his time and energy to the city of his birth.

D.J.B. & M.W.P.

December 1975

CONTENTS

PART I
ROMAN, ANGLO-SAXON, AND DANISH LEICESTER

PART II
MEDIEVAL LEICESTER

PART III
TUDOR AND STUART LEICESTER

PART IV
EIGHTEENTH AND NINETEENTH CENTURY LEICESTER

PART V
TWENTIETH CENTURY LEICESTER
by Jack Simmons

MAPS AND ILLUSTRATIONS

PART I

ROMAN, ANGLO-SAXON, AND DANISH LEICESTER

RATAE CORITANORUM

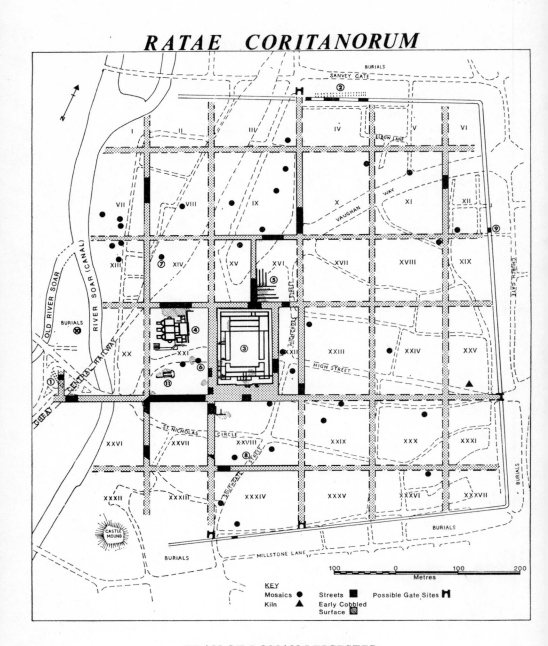

PLAN OF ROMAN LEICESTER

Section I

ROMAN LEICESTER

by Jean E. Mellor

Numbers in the text refer to sites marked on the plan opposite.

THE Roman name of Leicester, Ratae Coritanorum, tells us that during the Roman occupation the town was the capital of the Coritani, the Iron Age tribe whose territory covered the modern counties of Leicestershire and Lincolnshire and extended towards the Trent and the Nene. The Coritani show evidence of links with the Belgic tribes of the south-east in their pottery and in the fact that they issued coins, but side by side with this Belgic influence they also preserved a strong native tradition continuing from the earlier Iron Age.

There are no major sites in the area to help us to locate the pre-Roman capital of the tribe though Dragonby, Ancaster and Old Sleaford appear to have been important centres, the latter also being the site of a mint. Leicester itself has produced Belgic-type pottery and Coritanian coins but as yet no structures definitely assignable to the pre-conquest period have been identified.

There is no evidence that the Coritani resisted the Roman advance and by *c*. A.D. 47 most of their territory lay within the provincial frontier. Forts were established at tactical points within the tribal area including Leicester itself, though details of the military installation here are not clear. Military ditches have been found at West Bridge (1) and at Elbow Lane (2) but in neither case was it possible to discover any details of the size or nature of the fort. These two lengths of ditch may well represent successive phases in the military occupation of the site. The filling of the ditch at Elbow Lane contained pottery of Neronian date while the material from the ditch at West Bridge dated to the Flavian period. Excavations on other sites in the town, especially towards the west side and below the later civil rampart on the east and north, have revealed traces of timber structures and other features at the lowest levels, but in most cases the areas explored were either too small or too disturbed to determine whether the structures were of a military character or were to be associated rather with the civil development.

Following the decision, in the reign of Vespasian, to advance the frontier to the north and the consequent withdrawal of troops from lowland Britain, civil development and Romanisation in this part of the province began. In Leicester this followed the general pattern albeit slowly at first. The street pattern at Leicester appears to have been laid down towards the end of the first century; at West Bridge the military

13

ditch was sealed by the first street metalling. This evidence of town planning points to the fact that it was at this time that Leicester was formally constituted as the civitas capital of the Coritani despite the fact that the main public buildings were not provided until later. The central insula, later to be occupied by the forum, was now left vacant. It has been suggested that the reason for the delay in the construction of the public buildings in Leicester may have been that the territory of the Coritani was at first administered from the colonia at Lincoln, which was established c. A.D. 90, or that alternatively the tribe had been impoverished by the foundation of the colonia.

A spread of cobbling dating to this period has been recognised in the forum insula and those adjacent to it on the north, south and west (see plan). This could well have served as an open area for assembly and commerce prior to the construction of the forum. It may be that the area reserved for the forum eventually proved too large for the resources of the tribe. The street to the east of the forum is not part of the main street grid and was not constructed before A.D. 100-120 and it may be that this was a slightly later addition to the street plan following a decision to restrict the size of the forum and basilica.

By the beginning of the second century, then, Ratae already showed evidence of official town planning in the street system. It seems, however, to have developed mainly as a commercial centre at first as the only buildings so far known from this period, from excavations at Jewry Wall, Redcross Street and Blue Boar Lane, are shops and houses, basically timber-built and surrounding an open market space in the centre. During the hundred years following the accession of Hadrian the town was provided with at least three major public buildings and the growing prosperity of its inhabitants was also demonstrated in their private houses.

The sudden upsurge in the construction of public buildings began with the forum and basilica late in the reign of Hadrian and may have been prompted by the Emperor's visit to the province. The forum was basically an open space which acted as a market and a place of public assembly. This was surrounded on three sides by shops or offices with colonnades while the fourth side was occupied by the basilica, the law courts and centre of administration. It was the most important building in the town and usually occupied a central position.

In Leicester the forum and basilica (3) when finally completed occupied an area 132m x 91m although it did not fill the whole of the central insula. At the north end was the basilica with a nave 6.5m wide flanked by aisles 5m wide. Behind this were the offices of the local government officials, with an external portico beyond. South of the basilica the original plan seems to have conceived an open space surrounded by a double portico but the plan was changed before the building was finished. The internal portico on the west was divided into

14

a series of rooms and another portico was built on the inside. There has been little excavation of the east wing but its development was probably similar. When finally completed the south wing consisted of a double range of rooms with internal and external porticos. That the change of plan took place during construction is shown by the fact that offsets of walls belonging to both periods are sealed by the original floors.

At some stage there appears to have been a subsidiary entrance near the south end of the east wing though this was not matched by one on the west. The most likely place for the main entrance would have been through the south wing opposite the basilica and excavations here have revealed traces of what may have been a monumental porch although its exact plan is not clear. The street south of the forum is here expanded to more than twice its normal width and the effect of a gravelled open space at this point would have helped to make the entrance to the most important public building even more imposing.

The stone used in the building came mostly from local sources; granites from Groby, Enderby, Mountsorrel and Sapcote have been recognised, Swithland slate was used for the roof, and tile courses were found in those walls where some of the superstructure remained. For architectural features such as the columns and stylobate blocks millstone grit from Derbyshire was used. This material was worked on site as is shown by layers of crushed millstone grit which have been recognised in nearly all the forum excavations.

The next public building to be erected, probably closely following the completion of the forum, was the public baths, the foundations of which can still be seen at the Jewry Wall site (4). In this instance the insula had not been reserved and the bath-building, begun c. A.D. 145-150, replaced earlier shops and houses. Here also plans seem to have been changed while work was in progress and the building was not finally completed until c. A.D. 165-170.

The remains visible today do not represent the entire building. An exercise hall (palaestra) lay beneath St. Nicholas Church and would probably have been entered from the street to the east. This hall may have been open or roofed; foundations for a row of columns east of the Jewry Wall and parallel to it have been found and may represent either a portico round an open space or the internal division of a building. The baths were entered from the palaestra through the doorways in the Jewry Wall itself on either side of the central niche, which probably contained a statue. West of the Jewry Wall the foundations of the baths themselves are laid out and consist of a series of rooms heated to varying temperatures. Immediately west of the Jewry Wall, north and south of a central concourse, are two sets of three rooms which may have been changing rooms for men and women respectively. The central area between these two sets of rooms may also have served as a frigidarium (cold room). From here the bather passed into a further set of three rooms which were probably tepidaria (warm rooms); the most northerly one was certainly heated by a hypocaust. Beyond these rooms lay the caldaria (hot rooms). These had plunge baths extending beyond their outside walls; those on the west were heated by furnaces while those to the north and south were probably cold plunges. To the north the whole complex was screened by a portico but the boundaries to the south and west are less clear.

In the south-west corner of the site was a large square structure with strong internal walls which was obviously intended to bear a considerable weight. A drain was associated with this structure and it may have supported a reservoir. A public bath-building would require a regular supply of water and other drains on the site which are of massive construction suggest a heavy and continuous flow. The exact way in which this was maintained is not known but it has been suggested that the earthwork known as the Raw Dykes, south of Leicester, may have been an aqueduct bringing water to the city from the Knighton Brook. Although only a short stretch of this earthwork now remains it is known that it once extended much nearer to the city. On reaching the town the water could have been raised into a water tower and distributed from there to the baths and other buildings. In this connection a ditch with a square-cut channel in the bottom found on the north side of Friar Lane should be mentioned. The material in the filling was too late for it to be connected with the military occupation of Ratae but it could have held a wooden or lead water pipe although no traces were found.

Late in the second century or early in the third the last of the known public buildings was erected. Evidently by now the prosperity of the town had increased to the extent that the forum was no longer sufficient for its commercial needs and a secondary market hall (macellum) was built on the site of a derelict house of the earlier second century below Blue Boar Lane in the insula north of the forum (5). This building consisted of an aisled hall to the south, with an open space north of it enclosed by rows of shops or offices within colonnades. The plan is very like that of a forum and basilica and indeed the building was first identified as the principal forum of Ratae. However, its later date, smaller size, lack of tribunals and subsidiary position in the town plan all point to its being a secondary market hall.

The growing prosperity of the town and the increasingly Romanised way of life practised by its inhabitants is also evinced by the private houses which were being built from the beginning of the second century onwards. Only one of these has been excavated to any extent but others are known from a number of mosaic pavements recorded in the town. One of the finest of these dates to the middle of the second century and must have belonged to a wealthy member of the ordo (county council). This mosaic, known as the Peacock pavement, came from the same insula as the baths (6) and can now be seen in the Jewry Wall

16

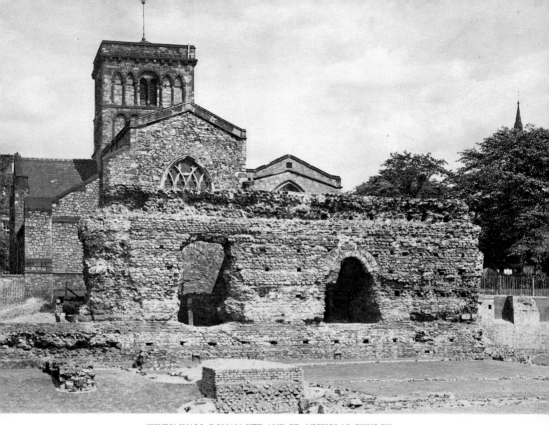

JEWRY WALL ROMAN SITE AND ST. NICHOLAS CHURCH

ROMAN AISLED BARN, NORFOLK STREET

ST. NICHOLAS' CHURCH: WINDOWS OF THE ORIGINAL SAXON NAVE REMAINING
ABOVE THE NORMAN ARCHES OF A LATER AISLE

ST. MARY DE CASTRO CHURCH: RICH NORMAN WORK ON THE NORTH SIDE OF THE CHANCEL

museum. Originally six metres square its design consists of nine octagonal panels framed with a twisted cable pattern. Eight of the panels contain geometric and floral designs while the central medallion shows a peacock with tail fully displayed. The 'eyes' of the tail are of blue glass tesserae and the mosaic also includes tesserae made from broken samian pottery which have enabled the pavement to be dated to the middle of the second century. Unfortunately it has not been possible to recover the plan of the house to which it belonged but the owners must have been both wealthy and sophisticated. An interesting detail in the design is in fact a mistake; the four corner panels are surrounded by a grey and white wave pattern which in three cases runs clockwise round the panel and in the fourth anticlockwise.

Another pavement worthy of note is the very fine geometric mosaic from Blackfriars, beneath the railway arch (7). This also consists of nine octagonal panels containing floral and geometric designs some of which convey an impression of whirling movement.

The most impressive of the private dwellings however is that on the Blue Boar Lane site which was superseded by the market hall (5). This house was originally built in the early part of the second century but later underwent extensive alterations as the prosperity of the owners increased. It was arranged round a peristyled courtyard and set back from the street to the south. During the alterations at least four rooms received mosaics but its most notable feature was the series of wall-paintings which decorated the walls facing onto the verandah round the courtyard. The design includes representations of architectural features such as niches and alcoves in perspective and also incorporates the more usual swags, garlands and candelabra with birds and winged cupids. Around one niche there is an elaborate architectural façade surmounted by a tragic theatrical mask, markedly similar to a wall-painting at Herculaneum.

The prosperity of this particular family however did not last long. By the end of the century the house was in ruins; part of it was evidently being used as a tannery or horn factory as a pile of cows' heads was found in a room which had once contained a mosaic, and obscene graffiti in Latin were being scrawled on the painted walls. The latter is in itself an indication of how far Romanisation had proceeded; most people scribble graffiti, obscene or otherwise, in their own language and not one which they have merely learnt at school.

Another house or shop on Southgate Street possessed a cellar (8). This is the only cellar of Roman date so far known in Ratae although they have been found in other towns. The cellar walls, which were still standing to a height of about two metres, had been plastered and painted white with narrow angle bands of red and blue. The cellar was entered through a narrow doorway and remains of two windows with splayed sills opening at ground level were found. In each of the walls was a rectangular recess which may have been divided by a shelf.

The exact area covered by the town in the second century is not known. Most towns of similar status were provided with earth banks towards the end of the second century but this does not appear to have been the case here. The known line of the medieval wall has been examined in several places, on the north, east and south sides of the town, and has everywhere been found to coincide with the Roman defences, which appear to have been constructed in the early third century. They consisted of a stone wall backed by a contemporary earth bank and with a ditch in front. The wall itself was almost totally robbed in the later medieval period but it seems to have been about three metres wide at its base although the foundations did not penetrate the natural sub-soil. Of the superstructure nothing is known. In a section at Butt Close Lane (9) the rampart, only standing to a height of about one metre, was found to consist of layers of gravel and turf, the individual sods of which were clearly visible. Two ditches have been found in front of the wall but these were re-cut and re-used in the medieval period.

The line of the defences of the Roman town from the third century onwards is known on three sides. The situation on the west side is not known. Excavations by the railway arches at West Bridge revealed street metalling which appeared to form part of a north-south street and to show that the grid system at one time extended so far to the west. This area might, however, as at Canterbury, have been excluded when the town was walled. Moreover, burials of apparently late Roman date found below the cloister area of the Austin Friars' site (10) suggest that this area lay outside the town walls although there was also evidence of some kind of occupation here in the later Roman period.

It is evident that the area walled in the early third century was slightly different from that of the earlier town. Earlier timber structures below the rampart in Butt Close Lane (9) were sealed by deposits containing second century material before the construction of the rampart, and an inhumation burial sealed by the rampart in Elbow Lane implies that this area was then outside the town boundary. Pottery kilns are also recorded from within the walls on the east side of the town and this industry was usually sited outside the towns. It is possible that a defensive system enclosing a somewhat different area has still to be found. Below the foundation trench of the town wall, between Millstone Lane and Friar Lane on the south, large post-holes and two gullies may represent the remains of an earlier palisade at this point.

The sites of the gates of the Roman town are not known for certain. If the street south of the forum, from which the building was entered, was the main east-west street carrying the Fosse Way through the town then the east gate should lie beneath its medieval successor near the Clock Tower. Heavy masonry recorded from below the Duke of

Cumberland Inn at Northgates may show that here too the medieval gate perpetuated the site of the Roman one. On the south side the Roman gate may have stood some 400 metres east of the medieval one which would bring it directly opposite the north gate. But here all is so far speculation. In the absence of any definite information about the western defences the site of the west gate is even more elusive. The Roman roads approaching and leaving the town—the Fosse Way which bisects the town from east to west, the road to Mancetter and the Gartree road to Colchester—are more precisely known further away from the town boundaries and can give us little guide to the accurate siting of the gates. From the Fosse Way at Thurmaston comes the Roman milestone which dates to the reign of Hadrian and gives the distance to Ratae—two miles.

The impression gained from the excavations so far is that by the third century the town had reached its full extent and that the rate of development had slowed down. This may be correct but it should be remembered that by far the greater part of the town has not yet been explored and that in many of the sites so far investigated the later Roman levels have been lost due to medieval and later disturbance.

During the late second and third centuries the public buildings were repaired and maintained. Floors were renewed in the bath-building and the forum and alterations were made to some rooms. In the late third or early fourth century further repairs and reconstruction followed a localised fire in the west wing of the forum.

Evidence for the kinds of religion practised in Ratae is scanty, although fragments of sculpture have been found which may indicate the sites of temples to the east of the forum. More is known of another building in the insula to the west of the forum (9), south of the public baths, which was constructed some time in the third century (11). The building is unusual in plan and is likely to have been a temple. It consisted of a narrow aisled structure some six metres wide and about 15 metres long on an east-west axis with transepts at the east end which cut across the aisles and terminated in apses. The building seems to have been entered from the west through a rectangular hall or courtyard of similar dimensions but lacking internal divisions. The floor level of the nave was sunk below that of the aisles and the walls of the nave were covered with red painted plaster. In the south wall of the nave was a small tiled recess which may have held a statue. A tile set vertically in the centre of the nave floor at the east end may hint at some kind of partition between the nave and the area to the east, possibly a sanctuary. The foundations of the external walls were packed with clay in places but this was not a consistent feature. The building sealed material of the late second and early third centuries and above the floor of the nave was a scatter of fourth century coins. Just south of the east end of the structure was a well the filling of which contained quantities of third

19

century pottery. The building has certain features in common with a Mithraeum but there is insufficient evidence for positive identification. Two small column bases and part of a carved male torso made from the local Danehills sandstone were found in the building.

In both town and countryside of the Roman Empire theatres are often associated with temples and religious enclosures but no structural evidence for either a theatre or amphitheatre has yet been found in Ratae. The presence of entertainers in the town is hinted at by the fragment of pottery which, if genuine, has the names of Verecunda (who may have been an actress) and Lucius, a gladiator, scratched on it.

Cemeteries are known to exist outside the town on all four sides, but little work has been done in these areas so far. Earlier finds include stone and lead coffins as well as cinerary urns of pottery and glass containing the ashes of the cremated dead. The practice of cremation was followed during the earlier part of the Roman occupation and was gradually replaced by inhumation. The fragment of the one tombstone found so far is too incomplete to yield much information.

Excavations have recently begun in the cemetery area to the west of the town. On a site near Great Holme Street three graves were excavated containing the remains of three individuals—two adults, male and female, and one adolescent. Behind the skull of the female lay a bone hairpin and hob-nails at the feet of the other two individuals indicated that they had been buried wearing boots or shoes. All three had been buried in wooden coffins which were also represented by the nails. Three late Roman burials have also been found at the Austin Friars' site; they were of an adult and two children. Both the infant burials were in shallow graves with no evidence of coffins. One of the children had been decapitated, and buried with the head between the femurs. This practice is known from other late Roman cemeteries and is thought to indicate Germanic influence.

One extra-mural building is known from Leicester. Its remains now lie below Norfolk Street near the junction of King Richard's Road and Fosse Road Central. The site was first discovered in the eighteenth century and subsequent excavations in the nineteenth century and in 1975 have revealed further information. Ranges of rooms lie on two sides of a central courtyard. Those on the west included mosaic pavements and opened off a corridor to the east. On the north side is another corridor at right angles to the first and presumably with a similar arrangement of rooms behind. South of the central area lay an aisled building which may have been a barn. No structures are so far known on the east side. The stages in the development of the site are not yet clear but pottery and coins dating from the first to the fourth centuries have been found. There are some signs of occupation below the central courtyard and this was itself reduced or divided at a later date by a wall towards the eastern edge of the area examined in 1975.

The prosperity of Leicester during the Roman period has already been discussed. The town acted as a market place for the surrounding area and like other towns in Roman Britain had wide trading contacts. A little is known of the industrial activities of its inhabitants. A possible tannery has already been mentioned. Pottery was also made locally as well as being imported and there is evidence for metal-working and glass-making. Ovens, hearths and slag are found on nearly all the sites excavated but the nature of the activity with which they were associated cannot always be defined.

This prosperity continued into the fourth century. Mention has already been made of reconstruction in the forum in the late third or early fourth century. Activity still continued in the market hall though of a rather dubious kind—in a corner of the courtyard silver was being illegally extracted from base silver coinage. This was a serious criminal offence and the fact that it was being carried on in a public place points to a certain laxity in law enforcement by this time.

During the later fourth century the defences of many towns were strengthened by the addition of bastions to the walls to support large catapults. As a part of this re-organisation the existing ditch was filled in and a new wider ditch was dug further out. It is possible that this happened at Leicester but the evidence for bastions is very slight. A second ditch has been found but due to its re-use in the medieval period close dating is not so far possible. Professional soldiers would have been needed to man the catapults and there is evidence that some towns were garrisoned by detachments of Germanic troops from the Roman army. Finds of certain kinds of buckles and strap-ends associated with military dress, which show strong Germanic influence, suggest the presence of such troops in Leicester. This is also suggested by the infant burial from the west side of the town. Saxon cremation urns are known from cemeteries outside the town and some of these are of early forms.

Romanised town life continued in Ratae until late in the fourth century. Towards the end of this period a fire destroyed parts of the forum, basilica and market hall and after this there was no reconstruction; the roof of the market hall was found where it had fallen. However, among the ruins at some later date a rough shelter had been constructed showing that life in Ratae still continued although it was of a very different character from that of the preceding three hundred years.

I should like to thank T. Pearce for re-drawing the plan of Ratae Coritanorum and J. S. Wacher for reading and commenting on the text.

FURTHER INFORMATION

The most recent full-scale treatment of British history in the Roman period is S. S. Frere: *Britannia* (2nd edition 1974). Two other recent books which have sections dealing with Leicester are M. Todd: *The Coritani* (1973) and J. S. Wacher: *The Towns of Roman Britain* (1975). All give bibliographies.

Ratae Coritanorum by E. Blank (1971) gives an illustrated account of Roman Leicester.

The principal published references to discoveries in Roman Leicester are:

Archaeological Journal, lxxv, Survey by Haverfield to 1918, with find-spots and references.

K. M. Kenyon: *The Jewry Wall* (1948). Excavations 1936-9 on the baths and Raw Dykes aqueduct.

Britannia, iv, The Forum and Basilica of Roman Leicester by Max Hebditch and Jean Mellor.

Transactions of Leicestershire Archaeological Society, xxviii, Summary 1939-51 by David T.-D. Clark.

Transactions of Leicestershire Archaeological Society, xxix, Excavations 1952 on north defences by R. G. Goodchild.

Transactions of Leicestershire Archaeological Society, xxxv, Interim report on excavations on Elbow Lane and Blue Boar Lane, 1958 by J. S. Wacher.

DATES FOR REFERENCE

A.D.	Period	Leicester
41-54	Claudian/Neronian	Establishment of a fort at Leicester
69-96	Flavian	Removal of garrison and establishment of Civitas capital
98-117	Trajanic	
117-138	Hadrianic	Construction of forum and basilica begun
138-192	Antonine	Construction of public baths
193-235	Severan	Construction of macellum and town walls
Third Century		Construction of temple (insula xxi) Public buildings repaired and maintained
Fourth Century		Presence of Germanic troops in garrison. Public buildings not repaired after fire

Section II

(a) THE LEGEND OF KING LEAR

(*As recorded by Geoffrey of Monmouth,*[1] *about* 1150)

[Geoffrey of Monmouth, a Benedictine monk and Bishop of St. Asaph, studied at Oxford and may quite possibly have visited Leicester himself, have seen the Jewry Wall or some other building and have noted the annual function—perhaps some sort of hiring fair—to which he alludes. His *History of the Kings of Britain,* from which this is an extract, was compiled partly from the traditions collected by Nennius (*fl.*796) and partly from Welsh or Breton manuscripts which are now lost; perhaps partly also from his own imagination. It is, at best, rather shaky evidence

[1] Bohn's Antiquarian Library:
Six Old English Chronicles
Edited by J. A. Giles, D.C.L. London, 1848.

that tradition connected the story of King Lear with Leicester before Geoffrey's day. Its main importance, perhaps, is the fact that the legend was accepted as serious history for the next four hundred years. The bulk of the story was translated from the Latin by Holinshed and incorporated in his Chronicle where Shakespeare read it. The translation given below is that of Dr. J. A. Giles.]

After this unhappy fate of Bladud, Leir, his son was advanced to the throne, and nobly governed his country sixty years. He built upon the river Sore a city, called in the British tongue, Kaerleir, in the Saxon, Leircestre. He was without male issue, but had three daughters, whose names were Gonorilla, Regau, and Cordeilla, of whom he was dotingly fond, but especially of his youngest, Cordeilla.

[Geoffrey then tells the familiar story of Lear and his three daughters at length, without further allusion to Leicester until the last paragraph which runs as follows:]

In the meantime Aganippus sent officers over all Gaul to raise an army, to restore his father-in-law to his kingdom of Britain. Which done, Leir returned to Britain with his son and daughter and the forces which they had raised, where he fought with his sons-in-law and routed them. Having thus reduced the whole kingdom to his power, he died the third year after. Aganippus also died; and Cordeilla, obtaining the government of the kingdom, buried her father in a certain vault, which she ordered to be made for him under the river Sore, in Leicester, and which has been built originally under the ground to the honour of the god Janus. And here all the workmen of the city, upon the anniversary solemnity of that festival, used to begin their yearly labours.

(b) TACITUS[1]
(c A.D. 97)

[The works of Tacitus are our principal literary source for the history of Britain during the half-century that followed the invasion of Claudius. This period included the almost successful rebellion of Boadicea, the reprisals and the consolidation of Roman power that followed, the subjugation of most of Wales and a victorious campaign in Scotland. Tacitus himself never visited Britain but his father-in-law, Cnaeus Julius Agricola, was the last of Vespasian's fighting governors and the hero of the battle of Mons Graupius in which the Scottish tribes were defeated. The Life of Agricola, which Tacitus wrote in addition to his general history (*Annales*), still leaves many details of administration and strategy tantalizingly obscure but it contains passages such as the following which may well be derived directly from the table-talk of the retired governor. Agricola had served in Britain for some years as a young man and came back to it as Governor in A.D. 78.]

[1] Bohn's Classical Library. *The Works of Tacitus* (The Oxford Translation, Revised). George Bell and Sons, 1882.

AGRICOLA; XIX, XX, XXI

The augmentation of tributes and contributions he mitigated by a just and equal assessment, abolishing those private exactions which were more grievous to be borne than the taxes themselves. For the inhabitants had been compelled in mockery to sit by their own locked-up granaries, to buy corn needlessly, and to sell it again at a stated price. Long and difficult journeys had also been imposed upon them; for the several districts, instead of being allowed to supply the nearest winter quarters, were forced to carry their corn to remote and devious places; by which means, what was easy to be procured by all, was converted into an article of gain to a few.

By suppressing these abuses in the first year of his administration, he established a favourable idea of peace, which through the negligence or oppression of his predecessors, had been no less dreaded than war.

The succeeding winter was employed in the most salutary measures. In order, by a taste of pleasures, to reclaim the natives from that rude and unsettled state which prompted them to war, and reconcile them to quiet and tranquillity, he incited them, by private instigations and public encouragements, to erect temples, courts of justice, and dwelling-houses. He bestowed commendations upon those who were prompt in complying with his intentions, and reprimanded such as were dilatory; thus promoting a spirit of emulation which had all the force of necessity. He was also attentive to provide a liberal education for the sons of their chieftains, preferring the natural genius of the Britons to the attainments of the Gauls; and his attempts were attended with such success, that they who lately disdained to make use of the Roman language, were now ambitious of becoming eloquent. Hence the Roman habit began to be held in honour, and the toga was frequently worn. At length they gradually deviated into a taste for those luxuries which stimulate to vice; porticos, and baths, and the elegances of the table; and this, from their inexperience, they termed politeness, whilst, in reality, it constituted a part of their slavery.

(c) ITINERARY OF ANTONINUS

[The 'Antonine Itinerary' was a road-book, probably official, of the Roman Empire. It has been called the Roman Bradshaw, but, in Britain at any rate it seldom lists the most direct route from one place to another. It may record the routes actually travelled by the official post-carriers or others who wished to call at the maximum number of settlements on the way. (A modern local bus-route is often equally indirect for a similar reason.)

The route which takes in Leicester is one of the two ways given from London to Lincoln. The other is by way of Colchester; the straight road through Castor is ignored.

M.P. stands for *milia passuum*, 'miles' of 1,000 paces, equalling 1,618 yards. The Romans presumably reckoned a pace from the fall of one foot to the fall of the same foot again, at a short marching step.]

ITER VI[1]

Item a Londinio Lindo	M.P.	CLVI.	[*sic:*]
Verolami	M.P.	XXI.	(St. Albans)
Durocobrius [*sic*]	M.P.	XII.	(Dunstable)
Magiovinio	M.P.	XII.	(Little Brickhill)
Lactodoro	M.P.	XVI.	(Towcester)
Isannavantia	M.P.	XII.	(Whilton Lodge)
Tripontio	M.P.	XII.	(Cave's Inn Farm)
Venonis	M.P.	VIII.	(High Cross)
Ratas [*sic*]	M.P.	XII.	(Leicester)
Verometo	M.P.	XIII.	(Willoughby on the Wolds)
Margiduno	M.P.	XII.	(Castle Hill)
Ad Pontem	M.P.	VII.	(East Stoke)
Crococalana	M.P.	VII.	(Brough)
Lindo	M.P.	XII.	(Lincoln)

(The modern identifications given are from the Ordnance Survey Map of Roman Britain. 'Isannovantia' is a misspelling of 'Bannaventa'—see Professor Haverfield's article in *The Victoria County History of Northamptonshire*, Vol. I. Names and distances vary widely in different sections of the Itinerary. ITER VIII (York to London *via* Lincoln and Leicester) gives:

Vernemeto	M.P. XII
Ratis	M.P. XII
Vennonis	M.P. XII
Bannavanto	M.P. XVIIII)

Section III

ANGLO-SAXON AND DANISH LEICESTER

In a town like Leicester the Roman period is, to all intents and purposes, a prehistoric age. Our knowledge of the city is almost entirely derived from the examination of excavated sites and material remains. For most of the Anglo-Saxon period the same is true but the remains are much fewer. For a long time, no written records make up for the loss. It is as if the moon, which showed us the outlines of buildings, had gone down; we grope in a black-out which is only relieved by points of light from the dimmed torches of hurrying strangers, none of them, unfortunately, going in our own direction.

The Midlands happens also to be the part of England where the darkness of the Dark Ages is most persistent. For the earliest period, Bede of Northumbria is our chief authority and the history of the later centuries was written under the inspiration of King Alfred of Wessex. The

[1] *Itineraria Romana*, Vol. I. *Itineraria Antonini Augusti et Burdigalense*. Ed. Otto Cuntz (1929), p. 73.

kingdom of Mercia, which included Leicester and which was dominant in the middle period, produced no great historian, or, if it did, his name and his writings were lost in the unrecorded sack of some Midlands monastery. To form any idea of life in Leicester between about A.D. 400 and A.D. 900 we must fall back on hints and scraps, eked out by a study of place-names and of such archaeological material as survives from the homes and graves of a people whose possessions were as simple as they were perishable.

The first Anglo-Saxons to reach Leicestershire were probably mostly Angles who came up the Welland from the Wash and perhaps up the Soar from the Humber. Some West Saxons may also have arrived fairly early by way of the Avon Valley and the Fosse Way. It is an open question whether, as they reached the limit of their thrust, they appeared as savage raiders and pillagers of a peaceful population or whether they came rather as hardy companies of pioneers, subduing the virgin forests to make their settlements, peaceable enough in intent but ready to defend their homesteads against raids by roving bands of savage aborigines. A third possibility is, of course, that they settled down side by side with, or were absorbed into, a continuing Romano-British society, but there is no positive evidence that this often happened.

It is not likely, however, that British elements were completely exterminated. In Leicestershire, Celtic roots survive in the names of Breedon, Charley, Charnwood, the River Soar, and interestingly enough, in the lowland village of Leire.[1] The earliest Saxon document (A.D. 803) in which Leicester is named, calls it *Legorensis civitas*. If Peatling does really mean 'the settlement of Poetla's people' this group may have been among the first to cross the watershed from the Welland, they may have found a British village on their flank, and they may have called the Roman town farther down the same valley 'the Ceaster of the people of Leire', and the name may have stuck in spite of British attempts to explain that it was properly called *Ratae*. It is also just conceivable that the legend of King Lear embodies a real tradition of a divided kingdom which might be an additional reason for the disappearance of the tribal name of the Coritani.

Whatever Celtic stock survived, it is doubtful if they retained any important elements of Roman culture. Roman provincial civilization had been too much a material, too little a spiritual thing for that. If its influence survived it was through the material reminders which it left. Pioneers in log cabins saw walled towns with great buildings of stone and realized that such things could be. In time they came to realize that such things could be useful; that walls were a protection against invaders and that monumental buildings would be worthy shrines for the faith that Augustine had brought back from Rome.

[1] Which may, however, represent a river name—Celtic river names are usually more persistent than village place-names.

26

In the meantime, settlements multiplied and a local trade began. It cannot have been long before Leicester was once more recognized as a convenient centre for the interchange of produce and as the residence of specialized artisans—the weaver, the miller, the blacksmith, the potter, the tanner, the wheelwright, and the jeweller. One characteristic, however, it did not have, and has not to this day. It was not and is not the natural capital of a homogenous tribe but rather the meeting-point of several different cultures. Angles from the Wash, Angles from the Humber, Saxons from Warwickshire, Mercians from the Trent, and Celts from the rocks and hills of Charnwood must have met, traded, and settled there.

The Mercians proper lay to the north and west of Leicester; they were originally the people of the Marches, perhaps of the boundary lands running from Cannock Chase to the Forest of Arden. In Leicestershire and south-east of it the people were known as the Middle Angles, a loose confederation of tribes which presently came under the domination of the Mercian king but even then was often ruled by a tributary king as a separate subject-state.[1]

Mercia remained pagan for some time after the conversion of Northumbria and it is from pagan burials that most of our Anglo-Saxon remains derive. They indicate a people with some skill in making large barbaric ornaments and a good deal less skill in pottery: we know very little about the woodwork and textiles which may well have been their best products.

The official conversion of the Middle Angles (something very different from an actual change of belief by individuals) took place in A.D. 653, some two hundred and fifty years after the effective end of Roman rule and perhaps a hundred and fifty years after the first Angles settled in Leicestershire. It came easily enough, following the marriage of the Middle-Anglian sub-king Peada to a Northumbrian princess. Anglo-Saxon paganism never seems to have been a positive or persecuting faith: the pillagers of monasteries and burners of towns were curiously like naughty children, ready to respond with sincere contrition to an authoritative rebuke. Their ready acceptance of Christianity was a sign that they were growing up, even if they did not all grow up into saints. The only things to which they clung tenaciously were their feasts and in these the Church wisely saw so little harm that it accepted some of them, notably Yule and Easter, without even a change of name.

After the conversion of the Middle Angles, Leicester begins to be mentioned, occasionally, in written history. Some, though not much, political and social importance is implied by the fact that it is named as the seat of the line of bishops of the Middle Angles which began soon

---

[1] Markfield—'the open land of the Mercians'—indicates that although there were Mercians in Leicestershire they were regarded by the bulk of the population as 'foreigners'.

after A.D. 670 though the diocese of Leicester was not finally established until A.D. 737. Even then it must not be supposed that Leicester was anything like a cathedral city as that was understood in Norman times. It is very doubtful if such things as a dean and chapter had been thought of and the bishop was, for a great part of the year, a missionary priest travelling round his diocese to baptize, preach, and prepare converts for confirmation. He had, no doubt, a central church of some importance. There is no harm in imagining that St. Wilfrid, a great founder of churches and monasteries, may have had something to do with its building, for he did, for a few years, administer the diocese. The discovery of rough stone foundations, cutting through the Roman work by the Jewry Wall, but themselves cut through by the later Saxon foundations of St. Nicholas' Church, gives at least a hint of its probable site.

Until well after A.D. 800, Leicester must have counted itself a lucky town. It was in the middle of the great Mercian kingdom which was at that time dominant. It may have been something of a local capital for both political and ecclesiastical affairs (though it is a wholesome corrective to any idea that these were closely centralized, to read of important meetings of English bishops at such places as Croft and Gumley). It was far enough away from a frontier to avoid changing hands as the unstable boundaries of the kingdom advanced and receded. For a long time the growing menace of Danish raids on the coast and into East Anglia can have been no more than a disturbing rumour. No doubt the young men of Leicestershire were called out from time to time for some successful or unsuccessful campaign; no doubt the town had its share of pestilences and destructive fires. No doubt refugees from less fortunate places were a recurrent problem, but disaster still held off.

It was between 865 and 874 that the whole structure of life in East Anglia and the Midlands collapsed. A great Danish army marched and pillaged up and down England until finally the whole of Mercia accepted a Danish nominee as king on the humiliating terms that the kingdom should be at the disposal of the conquerors as soon as they wished to occupy it. Three years later, in 877, Mercia was divided in half and a permanent settlement of Danes occupied the whole country as far west as the Watling Street. That most of Leicestershire came into the area of close settlement is quite clearly shown by the villages whose names end in the Danish terminations of -by and -thorpe and by names like Skeffington in which the English sc (pronounced sh) was changed into sk. (On the other hand, Shangton, only a few miles away, as well as Shenton, Sheepy, and Sharnford, on the western edge of the county, retained the old form.)

Leicestershire was so near the boundary that some of the wealthier people may have migrated with such possessions as they could carry. The bishop retired to Dorchester-on-Thames; it was to be more than a thousand years before there was again a diocese of Leicester. For the rest of the people the Danish settlement must have been a far greater disaster than the Norman Conquest, if only because it was a displacement that— as far as can be ascertained—extended to a lower level.

In Leicester itself, as opposed to Leicestershire, there may have been some mitigations to the disaster. From the point of view of the humble individual, a quick conquest may be less destructive than prolonged warfare, less ruinous than perpetual demands for ransom or tribute. Moreover, the Danish system of defence and domination was based on the establishment of fortified towns garrisoned by a local army and ruled by a jarl. Leicester, with Derby, Nottingham, Lincoln, and Stamford, became one of the 'Five Boroughs' of the Danelaw and as such was probably a good deal more important than it had ever been before. The fact must also have accentuated the existing difference between the relations of Leicester with what we now call Leicestershire and those of, say, Winchester and Exeter with their surrounding areas of country. As Sir Charles Oman puts it (*England before the Norman Conquest,* Chapter XXIV):

> When we contemplate the modern map of the shires between Humber and Thames, we recognize at once that we have to do with divisions much later and more artificial than those of Wessex. The first thing that strikes the eye is the uniform naming of the shires after their chief towns—of the seeming exceptions Rutland dates from after the Norman Conquest . . . Looking at the East Midland shires we note at once that they represent the Danish units of organization which Edward found and conquered. To the towns of Bedford, Northampton, Cambridge, Huntingdon, Derby, Nottingham, and Leicester we find appended an 'Army' and 'people owing obedience to the town', in the case of most of them a 'jarl' also is mentioned. It is hardly possible to doubt that the modern shire simply corresponds to the holding of the Danish 'army' which Edward subdued. The casual mention of the Chronicle that the lands 'owing obedience to Northampton' reached as far as the Welland, exactly describes the modern frontier of the shire . . . Under these new divisions, created by the Danes and taken over by Edward, as convenient units for his purpose, the old Mercian boundaries lay completely submerged. The ancient line between Gyrwas and Middle Angles, or South Mercians and Middle Angles, has no relation whatever to the tenth century limits between the tributary lands of one or another Danish 'army'.

Throughout King Alfred's long struggle to preserve Christian culture and to create the idea of national unity, Leicester was an occupied city behind the enemy lines. Danish forms of taxation and local government took root and persisted, but on the other hand it seems as though the English gradually infected their conquerors not only with their religion but with their loyalties. At any rate, when, in 918, the Lady Æthelflæd advanced into Danish Mercia, the army of Leicester laid down its arms and swore fealty to her so that she was able, according to tradition, to strengthen the town's walls and use it as a Saxon bastion.

The reconquest of Mercia was, on the face of it, only a temporary deliverance. It was followed by more Danish and Norse raids, by the humiliating and crushing tribute of the Danegeld, by the redivision of the kingdom and finally by the acceptance of Canute as King of all England. Something, however, had happened in the meantime. The men of the Danelaw, though they kept their own customs and their own language,[1] had become more or less Christian and rather more than less Englishmen. Canute was a foreign ruler, but almost in the sense that James I, William III, and George I, were foreign rulers: he did not, like William the Conqueror, impose domination by a foreign race. Had Canute's successors been of the same calibre as himself, and had the Normans been defeated at Hastings, England might have entered the Middle Ages as the acknowledged leader of a group of Northern States surrounding the North Sea and the Baltic.

This, however, is no more than a speculation on general history. Its only importance here is that it may help to make clear the background of life in an English city of the Danelaw in the last century before the Conquest. After years of crushing taxation, after wars and rumours of wars, culminating in the sack of the city by Edmund Ironside in 1016, Leicester had fifty years of peace and recovery. The exertions that had been made to raise a surplus for the payment of Danegeld or to replace the waste of war must have resulted in an agricultural production which could, in peace-time, support an increasing population in comfort. One may guess, from the map, that the old Fosse Way as well as the river served to carry goods from the Humber ports to the West Midlands and that, in the reverse direction, salt was brought down the Watling Street from Cheshire or across country from Droitwich. If so, Leicester was favourably placed for trade, particularly if, as is highly probable, there was a cross route, cutting off the High Cross corner and connecting Leicester more directly with the important towns of Tamworth and Lichfield. Connections with East Anglia may also fairly be assumed from the fact that they were so strong soon after the Conquest.

Trade of some sort Leicester certainly had. This is clearly indicated by the fact that, like other boroughs, the town had authorized moneyers who minted the royal coins stamped with their own name and that of the place of origin. But at the end of the Saxon period, trade was still only a sideline that just enabled a rather larger number of people to live in one place than could have been wholly supported by their work in the surrounding fields. Only nobles and priests at one end of the scale and slaves at the other followed what we should call whole-time occupations. Every man was his own carpenter, builder, furniture maker; every

[1] I am indebted to Dr. W. G. Hoskins for the information that Danish was a spoken language in Leicester market place in the late ninth and in the tenth and eleventh centuries; also that many Leicestershire surnames, e.g. Astill, Chettle, Nutt, Swain, and Herrick, are Danish in origin.

woman spun and sewed, baked, brewed, preserved food, and made clothes; first and foremost, even in the towns, every man and woman worked on the land. Leicester had three great open fields, known later as St. Margaret's, St. Mary's, and the West Field. One of them, or perhaps part of each, was sown every autumn with wheat and rye, another part of the land in the spring, with oats, barley, beans, and peas; a third part lay fallow. The meadows by the river grew a crop of hay and there was a still undefined area of forest from which firewood and timber could be freely drawn. Even if a man had begun to think of himself as a burgess and considered himself primarily a merchant or a manufacturer of goods for sale he would own and cultivate his strips in the common field and would turn out himself to cut and carry the hay and corn or to cart his household store of winter fuel.

Besides all this, he would take his part in the administration of customary law and in the settlement of local disputes. The free settlers of the Danelaw seem to have devised or brought with them a system which came nearer to self-government than that which obtained in the rest of England. There was a superior court or council of the Five Boroughs and a local court for each wapentake and each borough within the area. An innovation of far-reaching importance was the jury of presentment consisting of twelve thegns who swore on holy relics neither to accuse an innocent nor to protect a guilty person. (They could record a majority decision, though as, in this case, the minority were fined, unanimity was not improbable.)

Perhaps, at this time, Leicester had a population of fifteen hundred or two thousand people; about that of Queniborough or Market Bosworth to-day. Its buildings and their furniture were not much better than those of an Indian or West African jungle village, but to compare it with such a village would be wholly misleading. Its culture was not stationary; it was the product of five hundred years of growth and change. The Anglo-Saxons had found the Midlands a forest with a few clearings; the Normans found them a close patchwork of productive farms, backed by still enough woodland to provide plentiful fuel and building timber and grouped round hundreds of small villages with here and there a larger administrative centre such as Rothley or Melton Mowbray and with a fortified town like Leicester dominating and protecting the area of each shire.

It was a measure of the energy of Saxons and Danes, not only that the agricultural revolution had been accomplished but that, without the artificial foreign trade of Roman times, towns again performed a necessary function. It had not been an easy road to travel. The history of Anglo-Saxon England, as it was written at the time, is for the most part a rather depressing chronicle of foreign and civil wars, of the disturbed lives and often violent deaths of kings and saints, varied by brief notes of the famines, pestilences, diseases of cattle, and great winds that made particular years remarkable. Natural calamities like these were, in a locally organized community, more serious obstacles to progress than any wars or raids and it is rather important to remember that our ancestors spent a great deal more of their time in felling trees and cultivating the land than in fighting. Whole generations, in this part of England at any rate, were born and worked and died without seeing war at first hand, but few men can have gone through their lives without remembering disastrous harvests that brought countrymen and townsmen alike to the verge of starvation, without hope of relief from luckier areas.

Somehow or other, they got through it all, so that in 1066 England was, not for the first time, or the last time, seen to be rather more wealthy but rather worse equipped for warfare than her neighbours overseas. And, this time, it was no help to Leicester to know that the coasts where invasion threatened were both a very long way away.

FURTHER INFORMATION

The volume in *The Oxford History of England, Anglo-Saxon England,* by Professor F. M. Stenton, is a full and completely authoritative account of Anglo-Saxon and Anglo-Danish history and institutions.

England before the Norman Conquest, by Sir C. Oman is an excellent account of this as well as of the Roman period and brings out rather more clearly, for the general reader, the dramatic nature of the fluctuating struggles for personal and regional predominance.

The various histories of Leicester do little—indeed can do little—more than extract the few specific references to the town which are contained in these and other standard histories of England.

ANGLO-SAXON PERIOD

DATES FOR REFERENCE

General		Leicester	
A.D.		A.D.	
(About) 450	Earliest settlements in South (Hengist and Horsa?)	(About) 400 500	End of Roman Rule Probable early settlements
520?	Battle of Mount Badon		
(After) 550	Rise of Northumbria to supremacy		Confederation of Middle Angles
597	Mission of St. Augustine		Subordination to Mercia
664	Synod of Whitby	653	'Conversion' of Peada and Middle Angles
673-735	Life of Venerable Bede		
(From about) 700	Rise of Mercia to supremacy	691-702 737	St. Wilfrid in Mercia See of Leicester constituted
768-814	Charlemagne emperor of France		

32

General		Leicester	
A.D.		A.D.	
(From about)			
825	Rise of Wessex to supremacy		
871	Alfred's reign begins		
874	Danish conquest of Mercia	877	Leicester comes under Danish rule and Leicestershire is settled by Danes
901	Death of Alfred		
		918	Surrender to Æthelflæd
920	Reconquest of Mercia		
959-975	Edgar		Danish custom confirmed in Danelaw
975	Ethelred the Redeless Danish and Norse invasions	(After) 975	Reconquest by (foreign) Danes
1016	Canute King of England	1016	Sack by Edmund Ironside
1042	Edward the Confessor (Norman influences penetrate)		
1066	Battle of Hastings		

Section IV

ANGLO-SAXON BUILDINGS AND REMAINS

From the Anglo-Saxon, as from the Roman Period, one and only one building remains, in part, visible and above ground. The nave of St. Nicholas' Church was originally entirely Saxon: the Normans cut the lower portions into arcades of arches and threw out aisles beyond them. In the early nineteenth century almost the entire south wall was cut away so that the roof was supported on that side by one immense brick arch. The windows in the north wall are, however, typical Saxon work, and it is still just possible to visualise the sort of sturdy, simple building that stood on the site before the Conquest.

Other churches in Leicester claim a pre-Conquest foundation but it cannot be said that their present structure or even earlier underlying foundations present any clear architectural evidence to support such claims.

The lower walls of a stone building, which is almost certainly post-Roman and very possibly pre-Conquest, were uncovered in the nineteenth century during the building of premises in Guildhall Lane belonging to Messrs. Swain and were photographed at that time. Although the arched windows which might have helped to date the building have been destroyed, the main walls remain as the walls of a large coal cellar. An interesting feature is a series of cupboard-like

33

recesses in the walls, lined with Roman bricks. The windows, which were in the west wall only, may have opened into a courtyard extending as far as St. Nicholas Circle.

A considerable number of relics of the Saxon period have been dug up from time to time in Leicester and are preserved in the Jewry Wall Museum. The greater number of these are from burials of the Pagan period: objects of domestic use from the later periods have had less chance of escaping the acquisitive or destructive attentions of succeeding generations. Saxon objects in the museum have been so completely catalogued and described for the purpose of an exhibition[1] in 1946 that it is unnecessary to detail them here, but the introduction to the Leicester section of the Pagan period objects in the catalogue, which puts the whole position in perspective, may be quoted:

> Although somewhat meagre in quantity and quality, the finds of this period from Leicester and its suburbs are of historical importance. Indeed they represent the only sort of new evidence that we are likely to get for the life of the town in the Dark ages. Their scarcity in the area bounded by the walls of the Roman town—the hundred acres or so lying within the line of Sanvey Gate on the north, Churchgate and Gallowtree Gate on the east, Horsefair Street, Millstone Lane and the Newarke on the south and the river on the west—does not necessarily indicate extreme poverty and depopulation; the next three centuries are known to have been a period of progress in Leicester, yet they are no better represented. The contrast with the abundance of Roman finds from the town is apt to be misleading; the Roman layers, being the lowest, were the ones most protected by overlying rubbish from disturbance by medieval builders, and the collection of material from them has largely been reserved for an age of basement-making and of scientific curiosity. It may be that much archaeological evidence for the history and topography of Anglo-Saxon Leicester still lies under streets rather than under buildings in the centre of the modern city.

FURTHER INFORMATION

The Victoria County History; Leicestershire, Vol. I, has a good article on Saxon finds in Leicestershire. *Memorials of Old Leicestershire* (edited by Alice Dryden, 1911) contains an article by A. R. Horwood on 'Leicestershire in Anglo-Saxon Times'. These and the catalogue of the Anglo-Saxon exhibition referred to above, bring together most of the available archaeological and historical data.

St. Nicholas' Church is, however, fully described in a paper by Charles Lynam, F.S.A., read to the British Archaeological Congress in 1900 and reproduced in the *Leicestershire Archaeological Society's Transactions*, Vol. IX. This illustrates and discusses the Saxon windows in the north wall.

[1] City of Leicester Museum and Art Gallery: Anglo-Saxon, Leicestershire, and Rutland. Illustrated Catalogue (Prepared by F. Cottrill, M.A., Department of Archaeology, 1946).

PART II
MEDIEVAL LEICESTER

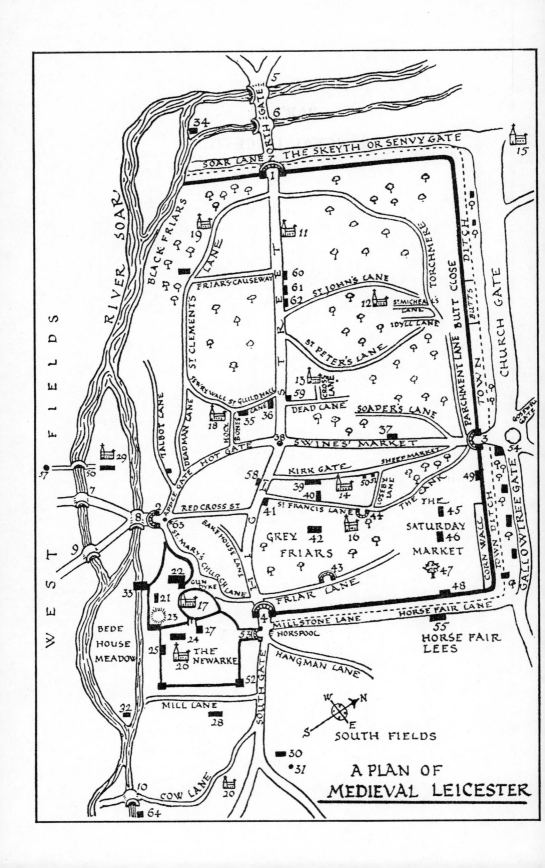

A PLAN OF
MEDIEVAL LEICESTER

KEY TO THE PLAN OF MEDIEVAL LEICESTER

1. North Gate
2. West Gate
3. East Gate
4. South Gate
5. North Bridge
6. Frogmire Bridge
7. Bow Bridge
8. West Bridge
9. Braunston Bridge
10. Cow Bridge
11. All Saints' Church
12. St. Michael's Church
13. St. Peter's Church
14. St. Martin's Church
15. St. Margaret's Church
16. Grey Friars' Church
17. St. Mary's Church
18. St. Nicholas' Church
19. St. Clement's Church
20. St. Sepulchre's Church
21. Castle Hall
22. Castle House
23. Castle Mound
24. Newarke Hospital
25. Dean of Newarke's House
26. Newarke College Church
27. Wyggeston's Chantry House
28. Newarke Grange
29. The Austin Friars
30. Hermitage
31. St. Sepulchre's Well
32. Newarke Mill
33. Castle Mill
34. North Mill
35. Old Mayor's Hall
36. Blue Boar Inn
37. Lord's Place
38. High Cross
39. Guildhall
40. Wyggeston's Hospital
41. Henry Costeyn's House
42. The Grey Friars' Priory
43. Grey Friars' Gateway
44. Grey Friars' Gateway
45. Shambles and Draperie
46. The Gainsborough
47. Elm Tree
48. Green Dragon Inn
49. Angel Inn
50. Maiden Head Inn
51. St. George's Guildhall
52. Rupert's Tower
53. Newarke Main Gateway
54. Bere Hill
55. Old Barn
56. Little Bow Bridge
57. St. Austin's Well
58. Roger Wygston's House
59. Free Grammar School
60. Shirehall
61. Prisona Regis
62. St. John's Hospital
63. Red Cross
64. Mary Mill

Section I

MEDIEVAL LEICESTER

In the medieval history of Leicester, two stories are interwoven, like the plot and underplot of an Elizabethan play. One may be compared with that of Roman Leicester: it is the story of how an outside stimulus gave the town an artificial grandeur. The other is more like that of Saxon and of modern Leicester: it is that of the gradual emergence and organic growth of municipal government and economic self-reliance.

The first story is the better known and the easier to tell. It may also be conveniently told first because it includes the chronology of definite local and national events which must be the background of any history. It is mainly the history of the Castle and its owners, the Norman and Plantagenet Earls.

What happened to Leicester at the actual Conquest is a matter of some doubt. *Domesday Book* records that the town contained 322 houses, and that there were 65 burgesses, who are listed as 'belonging' mostly to Hugh de Grantmesnil, but some to the King and a few to other Norman overlords. The Bishop of Lincoln held practically all the parish of St. Margaret's, outside the walls. Thompson, the nineteenth-century historian of Leicester, inferred from this that Leicester resisted the conquerors stoutly, that all but sixty-five out of more than three hundred burgesses were slaughtered and that the survivors were practically enslaved. Later historians have been much more impressed by the fact that only four houses are described as 'waste' or uninhabited and have supposed that it was not by any means every householder who, at or before the Conquest, ranked as a 'burgess'.

It would only be possible to assess the real position if we knew much more about the structure of society under the Saxons and, particularly, whether the Normans imposed a quite new system of tenure or whether they adapted a system which was already, in essence, feudal. On the whole it seems probable that 'the sack of Leicester in 1068' is a myth; that the Conquest was a disaster for the Saxon nobility, a crippling blow to the leading citizens and a rankling insult to every Englishman, but that the loss of life in the Midlands was small, and the break with tradition in local affairs by no means complete. Leicestershire certainly suffered nothing like the Conqueror's dreadful 'harrying of the North' which is said to have left no living being between York and Durham.

Material disasters, however, came soon enough to Leicester and though it was perhaps important that they were delayed until adjustment to the new order had been quietly accomplished, they probably robbed us of some notable Roman, Saxon, and early Norman buildings which might otherwise have survived. A Norman town, even if the citizens were allowed some latitude in managing their own affairs, was, in the last resort, the personal property of its overlord: if he waged private war, he or his opponents might plunder it, if he rebelled against the king, the sack of his town was the first and easiest step to take against him. Leicester was sacked or plundered three times in a hundred years and the last time was the worst. Because, far away in Normandy, Robert Blanchesmains, Earl of Leicester, was in revolt against Henry II, Leicester, after a three weeks' siege, was taken and laid waste by the King's Justiciary. The parish of St. Michael (between All Saints' and St. Margaret's) seems, in particular, to have suffered a lasting depopulation. Many of the richer citizens paid a heavy fine to be allowed to return to the Earl's other towns of St. Edmundsbury and St. Albans. The Castle held out but was later surrendered and its defences thrown down. The Earl himself, who had landed in Suffolk, was defeated and captured but, after a short imprisonment, was graciously pardoned.

The last fact may have been cold comfort to those who were trying to rebuild their lives among the ruins of Leicester, but it was a guarantee that the town, if not the fortunes or the dwellings of individuals, would quickly rise again to prosperity. A Norman Lord, like a Roman Governor, could have an important town almost wherever it suited him to establish one and could nourish it at his pleasure from the produce of the wide-spread lands that owed him tribute. Like the Romans, and unlike the Saxons, he chose to spend a high proportion of this tribute in buildings of enduring stone. In Leicester, during the century that had already passed since the Conquest, six churches had been either founded or replanned, the great abbey of St. Mary de Pratis[1] had begun to rise, and a noble hall had been built beside the Castle keep.

All these survived or were rebuilt. All, and particularly the Castle and the Abbey, were sources of spending power, bringing money in from outside the town and providing employment within it for a host of small tradesmen and artificers.

It so happened that the Earl of Leicester was, from the first, a very great man; that is to say, a very wealthy and powerful one. It also happened that, out of his numerous estates, he usually chose Leicester as his personal headquarters. This, with the foundation of the Abbey, more than made up for the fact that the rents and fees which, on any reasonable basis of church organization, should have served to refound and re-endow the old bishopric of Leicester, went instead to swell the enormous revenues of the Bishop of Lincoln whose suzerainty over a suburb was for a very long time an awkward complication for Earl and burgesses alike.

---

[1] The Abbey was founded by Robert le Bossu, first Earl of Leicester, in 1143. He was probably the best of the Norman earls, a learned and pious man as well as an able statesman.

The Norman overlords of Leicester (styled Earls after 1118) were successively the de Grantmesnils, the de Beaumonts, and the de Montforts, the transfer from one family to another being effected by influence, sharp practice, a claim resting on marriage with the female line, or a combination of all three. After the sack in 1173, Leicester had quiet under their protection and patronage for nearly a century. There was, presumably, a lean time under Simon de Montfort the elder and in the early days of his famous son, for during that time the Earl was an absentee and for part of it his estates in England were held in nominal trust by the Earl of Chester. Simon the younger, however, married Henry III's sister, was confirmed in his inheritance and proceeded to bring to the Earldom of Leicester a brief period of national importance. His career as leader of the barons and as virtual dictator after the defeat of the King at Lewes is a matter of national, not of local, history. There is no record that burgesses from Leicester were among those whom he, for the first time, summoned to Parliament and probably his townsmen were grateful if they were excused attendance. To them he was a kindly and considerate overlord who could spare time from national pre-occupations to hear and, for a suitable consideration, grant, petitions for the remedy of long-standing grievances. He did not give Leicester the land which is now the Victoria Park, any more than he anticipated nineteenth-century ideas of popular self-government, but he did, inside and outside of Leicester, listen to the voice of the English people and the English people venerated his memory as the first great man whom they could call their champion.

When de Montfort fell at Evesham his lands and title were given by Henry III to his own son Edmund Crouchback. It was a false move on the King's part; the Lancastrian earls, being even richer than their pre-decessors and of royal blood as well, were potentially or actually nothing less than a standing menace to the Crown. To Leicester, however, their frequent presence brought prosperity and distinction. It is recorded that the household expenses of Thomas of Lancaster in 1313 amounted to £7,309 in a year, equivalent perhaps to £2,125,000 of modern (1976) money. Not nearly the whole of such an expenditure would—or could —have been spent in one place, but any Earl who made Leicester even an occasional headquarters must have provided tradesmen with pickings that far more than balanced the 'presents' to influential people at the Castle which are so frequently recorded in the municipal accounts.

Three of the Lancastrian earls were mainly resident in Leicester during their later years—Henry of Grosmont who died in 1345, Henry, first Duke of Lancaster, who died in 1361, and John of Gaunt who died in 1399. Not only did they keep great state at the Castle but the first founded and his successors enlarged and endowed the collegiate church and its associated hospital in the Newarke—Earl Henry's New Work. With John of Gaunt's death the story of the Earls of Leicester comes to an end, for on the accession of his son as Henry IV the title and estates were absorbed in the Crown.[1] Princely expenditure and princely charity no longer centred in Leicester; only occasional royal visits and the ecclesiastical foundations remained to make Leicester still rather different from other county boroughs, still rather richer than other Midland market towns.

The ecclesiastical foundations, however, were by now important enough in themselves; perhaps they were the most important element in the medieval life of the town. One of the most astonishing things about medieval England is the amount of labour and skill that could be devoted by such a small and poor population to the 'unproductive' work of building and serving churches and monasteries. The answer can only be that the work was willingly, even joyously, undertaken by all. It is here that any analogy with Roman building breaks down completely. A castle, certainly, might be built by forced labour, and a grim ugly thing it generally was, but an abbey or a parish church grew and looked like a living thing, springing out of the self-sacrifice of baron, burgesses, and villeins alike. It would be quite wrong to turn from one aspect to the other of the economic and social life of Leicester without pausing to note the great spiritual, artistic, and material achievement of the medieval church.

It is not at all easy for us to realise the extent of that achievement. Most of the buildings that would help us have vanished. Not a stone remains above ground of the great abbey, with its cathedral-like church, of the collegiate church in the Newarke, of the friaries of the Dominicans, the Franciscans, and the Augustinians. The old churches of St. Peter, St. Michael, St. Sepulchre, St. Clement, and St. Leonard have gone; those of St. Nicholas, St. Mary, St. Margaret, All Saints, and St. Martin remain but they no longer throng and dominate a tiny, rather squalid, walled town in a wide expanse of meadow and woodland.

What is even more difficult to reconstruct is the background of living conditions that made the buildings and all that went on in them seem worth while; the lack of books, of pictures, of variety of food, the impossibility of escaping in any way from one's immediate environment and daily round except through war or the service of religion. If we could realize all that, we should understand the medieval builders, the monks and the pilgrims; we might even begin to understand the Crusades.

The Castle and the Abbey, overlooking Leicester from opposite corners, symbolized the two powers, feudal and clerical, that stabilized the medieval system. In the end, the central government of the Tudor Kings brought them both to the ground, but this could never have happened without anarchy if something had not grown up in the towns to take over many of their functions.

[1] The Chancellor of the Duchy of Lancaster, by virtue of this connection, still appoints the Masters of Wyggeston's Hospital and Trinity Hospital.

The feudal system worked beautifully on the country manors for which it was devised; in the towns it was, from the start, an inconvenient arrangement for all concerned. Where all the inhabitants could form a single crowd in the market place, it was hopeless to expect some of them to be loyal to the Bishop, some to the Earl, some directly to the King and a few to the lords of distant manors. Their real loyalty was to one another and to their birthplace; it very soon became easier to deal with them as a corporate body and to hold a few of the leading citizens responsible for the good behaviour of them all. Naturally, no overlord was content to be a financial loser by such an arrangement, but each one, as he succeeded to his title, was prepared to strike a bargain. Instead of collecting individual tolls he would accept a guaranteed annual rent; for a lump sum down he would give or restore rights of jurisdiction in commercial cases, sometimes 'for the good of his soul' and for peace and quiet he would even make a free gift of some coveted liberty—particularly if it cost him nothing.

The history of these bargains is preserved in a succession of charters which it was very much in the townspeople's interest to retain, because if by any accident the charter was lost or mislaid it would be quite possible for the Earl's agent to deny that its provisions held good. (This, according to their own story, actually happened to the burgesses of Leicester on one occasion and led to the reimposition of a tax called gavel-pence which had been remitted.)

It was fortunate for historians that the charters were so important to the citizens. It was much more fortunate for the rest of us that a responsible body of citizens to negotiate them was important both to them and to their overlord. Very early—perhaps within fifty years of the Conquest—there seems to have been a body of twenty-four 'jurats' in Leicester, led at first by two aldermen, but later by a mayor, who acted for the burgesses and effectively controlled the town's internal affairs. Through these men the Earl or his steward could conveniently deal both with the Portmoot, which included all burgesses, and with the Gild Merchant, which included all licensed traders, some of whom lived in the suburbs and were not burgesses.

The evolution of the complicated system of local government which was finally developed in medieval Leicester has been traced in careful detail by recent historians.

In comparison with other towns of similar status, Leicester was very slow to press for a full charter which would enable the corporation to collect all the Lord's dues themselves and pay him a fixed rent instead. This may well have been because the relations of the burgesses with the Earl and his steward were, for the most part, unusually friendly. They were not by any means behindhand in seeking or obtaining relief from individual imposts or disabilities which were found irksome and the mayor and jurats exercised in practice quite as full executive powers as the corporations did elsewhere. The important general point is that in Leicester as elsewhere a system of government by representatives (though they were, in a large measure, self-elected representatives) was hammered out and that it resulted from the initiative of the citizens themselves.

Only here and there have odd details of the medieval system survived to affect life in Leicester to-day. The office of High Bailiff, rare in a modern city, reminds us of the watching brief held by the Earl in civic affairs long after he had renounced active intervention. The City Arms display the Cinque-foil which was the badge of Robert Fitz-Parnel, the last of the de Beaumont earls and the Wyvern which was the crest of Thomas of Lancaster. Of more practical importance are the Wednesday and Saturday markets which were instituted so that the country people could bring their produce in for sale and which, with the periodic fairs, provided exceptions to the general rule that only burgesses might trade in the town without paying heavy tolls.

The main structure of medieval town governance was, however, too closely linked to that particular state of society to have been capable of adaptation to what we regard as the normal conditions of modern life. Medieval laws and by-laws were framed to meet circumstances much more analogous to those which we have experienced only under the exceptional conditions of major wars—shortage both of raw materials and of finished goods, constant danger of real famine, the necessity of keeping a high proportion of the population at work on the production of the bare necessities of life. Viewed in this light, price-fixing regulations such as the assize of bread, restrictions such as that which limited liberty of trade to members of the Gild Merchant and measures against 'regraters and forestallers'—the potential profiteers of those days— seem understandable, even familiar. Examined individually, such measures prove to be as different from those of to-day, or yesterday, as the Statute of Labourers was from the war-time Essential Work Order, but in essence they were shots at the same target of fair shares and fair prices in a closed economy.

Some of the old documents, on the other hand, are interesting not because they can be compared with anything of which we have recent experience, but because they remind us that the medieval town was still linked, or was only just breaking its links, with earlier communal systems. When the burgesses fought (as they were obliged to do repeatedly) for their rights of pasturage in the Cowhay,[1] they were not thinking of themselves as mercers or glovers, weavers or wool-merchants, but as tenants of the manor on whose common rights the Lord's enclosed demesne threatened to encroach. In the words of G. M. Trevelyan (*English Social History*, Chapter II):

[1] Outside the South Gate, on the Aylestone Road.

In the fourteenth century the English town was still a rural and agricultural community, as well as a centre of industry and commerce. It had its stone wall or earth mound to protect it, distinguishing it from an open village. But outside lay the 'town field', unenclosed by hedges, where each citizen-farmer cultivated his own strip of cornland; and each grazed his cattle and sheep on the common pasture of the town, which usually lay along the river side.

A relic of something much earlier than the manor, earlier, probably, even than the three-field system of farming, was the curious custom of Borough English under which the youngest son inherited his father's estate. No one can say for certain what its origin was, but it was a system which may have been sound enough when families were pioneers in a limitless area of virgin forest. Then, with an axe and a yoke of oxen, each son as he grew to manhood could carve a clearing and found a family for himself, leaving the youngest and weakest to take over the cleared but partly exhausted paternal acres. Things had changed very much when, in 1255, the burgesses of Leicester petitioned for a reversal of the system 'for the common utility and improvement of the state of the same town, which on account of the feebleness and youthfulness of the heirs, for a long time past has almost fallen into ruin and decay'. The security of the town and of its established businesses was now more thought of than the encouragement of a pioneering spirit.

Security in a stable society was, in fact, the watchword of the Leicester burgesses. Quite enough things could happen to a comfortable tradesman without his trying to make things happen, and most of the things that could happen were very unpleasant indeed—bullying and extortion from above, risings of peasants from below, bad harvests, destructive tempests, and pestilence. Battle, murder, and sudden death in this world, eternal damnation in the next, were not at all remote possibilities. So, most of his energies, after he had seen to the ordering of his own and the town's daily affairs, were devoted to providing, as best he could, against these last contingencies. With his fellow-craftsmen he formed or joined one of the many Gilds which supplemented the all-embracing Gild Merchant. In their first intention, these were primarily religious bodies; the Gild of St. George, The Gilds of Saints Mary, Margaret and Catherine, The Gild of St. John, of the Assumption, of St. Michael, of the Trinity, and, chief of all, the Gild of the Corpus Christi. In practice, the Gilds were friendly societies, burial clubs, and occasions for annual feasts and ceremonies as well as organizations responsible for paying chantry priests to say masses for the souls of departed members. The procession on Corpus Christi Day and the Riding of the George[1] became the most notable events of the year, dignified by every appurtenance of

[1] In the Corpus Christi procession, choristers and civic dignitaries followed priests carrying the Host.
The Riding of the George was a pageant in which a figure of St. George, mounted and in armour, was paraded round the town, followed by the Dragon.

civic pomp, joined and enjoyed by the whole population. The religious Gilds thus fulfilled a broader purpose than the earlier associations of particular occupations which were primarily, though not exclusively, concerned with the regulation of trade practices.

Gradually the Corpus Christi Gild became so much identified with the chief people of the town, it became so much a matter of course for the Mayor and Corporation to head it, that, when the old Hall of the Gild Merchant became too shabby and was found too small for them, they used, and eventually bought, the Corpus Christi Hall which, with a good many alterations, served their purpose until 1875 and was even then fortunately not demolished.

Many aspects of medieval life were seen at their best in its latest period. Others were still a long way from reaching the best that could be attained within the framework of a medieval society. England, by Continental standards, was a young country and had much to learn. The application of architectural and constructional skill to the town dwelling-house had hardly been thought of. Furniture was still a matter of tables, stools, and a few oak chests. The first great English poet was a protégé of Leicester's last Lancastrian earl. The art of painting was beginning to make strides forward in the reign of Henry VI. And yet, in other respects, we can see now that the medieval garment was worn out long before it was finally discarded. By 1300 the feudal system was no better than a patchwork with more exceptions than rules. Fifty years later the Black Death disturbed beyond full recovery the already unstable equilibrium of economic and social life. Labour became scarce and dear, peasants revolted, farmers began to turn from producing corn for local needs to sheep and cattle ranching.[1] Leicestershire sent more and more wool to be sold in Calais and woven on the continent. As this and other overseas trade developed the seaports grew in importance at the expense of inland towns and merchants of the Staple of Calais became richer and more powerful than most manorial lords.

Farmers had been rudely forced to change their methods; the old local manufacturing trades in towns like Leicester were entering a long slow period of decline. Something worse was happening to the Church; it was suffering from fatty degeneration. Here again the Black Death must be held partly responsible. It had hit both friars and parish priests particularly hard, for they had not shirked their duty of visiting the sick.

[1] This was the general picture, but revolutions in England are seldom either sudden or complete. On the one hand there is evidence that Leicester merchants were wool traders even before 1300. On the other hand, in spite of numerous enclosures, Thomas Tusser could still, in 1571, cite Leicestershire as a typical 'champion' or open-field county:

> 'Example by Leicestershire,
> What soil can be better than that?
> For anything heart can desire,
> And yet it doth want, ye see what.
> Mast, covert, close pasture and wood
> And other things, needful as good.'

There is ample evidence that a period followed in which the shortage of scholars caused a dreadful lowering of standards. Anyone who could scrawl his name and stumble through a Latin prayer could gain admittance to an easy living from the revenues that flowed in as smoothly from a sheep farm as from a populous parish. Lollardry was a natural reaction and if merry Dan Chaucer was one of John of Gaunt's protégés, stern John Wycliffe was another. In fact, for the last hundred years of the Middle Ages, the Church, one of the twin pillars that had supported the system, was slowly rotting; and when the other pillar, the Baronage, had been whittled away by the War of the Roses, it only needed a hard push to send the whole structure crashing about the heads of peaceful burgesses.

But the danger was not one that could be foreseen, any more than it could be averted, by such men. Moreover, if the finest flowers of the medieval garden had begun to fade by about 1350 there were many late blooms and sunny days to come. Midsummer was past, but winter was still far away.

The Black Death—of which the worst outbreaks occurred in 1348 and 1361—hit Leicester hard. In the second of these Henry, Duke of Lancaster, died, and of the first epidemic, Henry of Knighton, a monk in Leicester Abbey, wrote that in three parishes alone, fourteen hundred people perished 'and so in all the parishes in great multitudes'. His statistics, which would imply at least two thousand deaths out of a population of about six thousand, must not be taken too seriously, but he was a contemporary and there is no doubt that the loss of life was grievous and bereavement universal. Yet society, on the surface, was curiously little affected. Entries to the Gild Merchant maintained their numbers if not their quality and there was no break in the continuity of the Gild of the Corpus Christi which had been founded in 1343, only five years before the first Black Death.

Looking a little deeper, however, one can see signs of a long period of trade depression. New building or rebuilding of churches stopped. In 1445, in spite of the royal need for money to support the French wars (no longer, as had at first been the case, self-supporting or better) Leicester's tax quota had to be cut by more than 20 per cent. And the Corpus Christi Gild, in the first forty years of its existence seems to have lost almost all its original income so that it had to be re-endowed by a new set of benefactors in 1392.

Yet, as we can realize by thinking of the 1930's, a trade depression following heavy loss of life and a considerable social upheaval neither means that every individual is worse off and more miserable, nor prevents the extended use of new inventions and technical developments that make life more convenient and more varied for all classes.

Leicester may have been relatively stagnant, in spite of some moderately successful efforts to revive the manufacture of woollen goods and to make the town a minor centre for the marketing of raw wool. But her citizens shared in the general advances that, especially in towns, took place in the social life of England. Printed books, and the new ideas that they contained, were just beginning to circulate in the fifteenth century; the English language was becoming stabilized and some laymen were finding it worthwhile to learn to read and write. Ingenious men, no longer fully occupied in constructing churches and castles, learned to put a second storey and a chimney into a citizen's private house. House-holders and their wives might consider themselves badly off but they could and did buy things for their homes which had been unknown, or laboriously home-made, in the relatively prosperous days of the thirteenth century. A Leicester 'mercer' in the fifteenth century had amongst his stock (besides such raw materials as wool, wool-fells, and skins) gowns in taffeta or silk, daggers, bowstrings, harpstrings, writing-paper, materials for making ink, vegetable seeds, twenty different kinds of British and Paris silk, children's stockings, silk coifs and kerchiefs for nuns, knives, candelabra, coal-scuttles, horseshoes, honey, raisins, and salt.[1]

In one respect Leicester was, compared with other inland towns, fairly fortunate. After John of Gaunt's death in 1399 there was no resident Earl, but the Castle was still kept up by its royal owners, and frequent visits of the court, though they were expensive in presents and civic feasts, brought their reward on colourful pageantry. Henry VI, the founder of Eton and of King's College, Cambridge, was, as a small boy, knighted in Leicester after keeping his vigil in the Church of St. Mary de Castro. Parliament met in Leicester in 1414, 1426, and 1450. Occasions like these gave opportunities for long-headed burgesses to suggest that rather more power might be given to a loyal corporation, that some tax might be conveniently compounded, that an additional fair, under charter, would be profitable to all concerned. Less commercially minded men, the forebears of Nick Bottom and Peter Quince, would prepare a miracle play of special splendour when it was to be seen by burgesses from other towns and might possibly bring local talent to royal notice and favour. And perhaps when the king went back to the capital a few adventurous youngsters, despairing of opportunities in sleepy Leicester, managed to attach themselves to his retinue and went, like Dick Whittington, up to London to see whether it was true that there the streets were paved with gold.[2]

[1] Cited by Dr. S. Thrupp in an article on the Grocers of London in *English Trade in the Fifteenth Century*, edited by Eileen Power and M. M. Postan. (It is necessary to say, however, that this particular tradesman's enterprise may have been exceptional and was apparently ill-rewarded: the reason we know so much about his stock is that he went bankrupt.)

[2] Medieval people not only travelled a good deal, but often settled in another town for life. The names of Joh. de Wynchelsee, Rog. de Dancastre, Will. de Grantham, Ric. de Preston, Tho. Brown de Wircester, and Rob. de Swafham, occur in a single Leicester Merchant Gild Roll (1364-5). It would be interesting to trace the description 'de Leicester' in the records of London and other towns.

So, through the confused and purposeless period of political history that begins with the glorious but unprofitable battle of Agincourt and continues with the less glorious and equally unprofitable battles of the Wars of the Roses, life jogged on in Leicester with perhaps rather more than the normal head-shakings over the degeneracy of the times, the incompetence of officials and priests, the pleasure-loving ways of young people and the dangerous spread of heretical views, but with no realization that an epoch was coming to an end. Just before it did so, medieval Leicester was granted a little Indian summer of prosperity. Some turn of commercial practice seems to have diverted a larger share of the profits of the wool trade to the town; leading citizens built themselves good houses and the money was available to carry out the long-projected rebuilding and beautifying of St. Margaret's Church.

When in 1485, Richard III spent a night at the 'Blue Boar', rode out over Bow Bridge, a crowned king, to Bosworth Field, and came back, a naked corpse, thrown across a horse, it was, for Leicester, a dramatic episode, and one that seemed likely to terminate those tiresome wars which ephemeral kings and ambitious barons had conducted up and down the countryside though not, fortunately, very greatly to the annoyance or detriment of townsmen. But, in fact, the accession of Henry VII, beginning the strong rule of the Tudor monarchs, was to spell the doom of the particular state of society that made it possible for towns to be organized and to flourish on a medieval basis. The Indian summer would go on for a little longer, but the nights were drawing in; there was an evening chill in the air. And if, about that time, any thoughtful citizen looked out towards the Forest he may have noticed that, not only metaphorically but also quite literally, fuel was getting short.

FURTHER INFORMATION

No attempt will be made, in this or in succeeding sections, to give a list of important general works which have been, or should have been, consulted. G. M. Trevelyan's *English Social History* must, however, be mentioned as providing the most useful of all backgrounds for the periods with which it deals.

Local histories become important in the medieval period. The chief of them are:

John Nichols: *History and Antiquities of the County of Leicester* (8 vols. in 4. London, 1795-1811). A vast compilation which includes all or practically all that was known about Leicester and Leicestershire at that time. The earlier narrative by William Burton (1622) is reprinted in full.

John Throsby: *History of Leicester* (Leicester, 1791). Just previous to Nichols and used largely by him. Chiefly important for its records of archaeological discoveries and of events within the writer's recollection. Interesting to read, but ill-arranged and poorly indexed.

James Thompson: *History of Leicester* (Leicester 1849). The first readable history on chronological lines. Thompson made extensive use of the Borough records which he searched and translated. His facts are generally

MEDIEVAL WING AT
THE REAR OF ROGER
WYGSTON'S HOUSE. A
GLIMPSE OF LEICESTER
BEFORE THE GENERAL
INTRODUCTION OF
BRICK BUILDINGS AT
THE CLOSE OF THE
SEVENTEENTH
CENTURY

ST. MARGARET'S
CHURCH: FIFTEENTH
CENTURY TOWER

THE GUILDHALL:
A MEDIEVAL BUILDING
WITH SIXTEENTH- AND
SEVENTEENTH-CENTURY
ADDITIONS

MEDIEVAL PACKHORSE BRIDGE AT AYLESTONE

accurate but his accounts of medieval institutions require some correction in the light of later scholarship.

Records of the Borough of Leicester. Edited by Miss E. M. Bateson. An essential source-book used by all later historians. Each volume is introduced by a scholarly and readable essay.

Mrs. T. Fielding Johnson: *Glimpses of Ancient Leicester* (Second Edition with supplementary notes, Leicester, 1906). An eminently readable and beautifully illustrated popular history. As far as the medieval period is concerned the author relies on the histories already enumerated.

C. J. Billson: *Mediæval Leicester* (Leicester, 1920). Not a chronological history but a most important series of essays on medieval topography, buildings, markets and townsmen. Billson is thoroughly trustworthy and very readable. There is a very full bibliography which is most useful and the book is illustrated with excellent photographs, drawings and maps.

S. H. Skillington: *A Short History of Leicester* (London, 1924). Most valuable for its concise account of medieval institutions of which the author made a special study. Entirely reliable except in rare cases where fresh facts have come to light since it was written. The same author's other works, notably *The Trinity Hospital* and *The Old Town Hall* carry his investigations further and the latter work includes a very clear and full account of medieval gilds.

Mrs. F. E. Skillington: *The Plain Man's History of Leicester* (Leicester, 1950). It is convenient to notice the book here, though it deals with all periods and is particularly interesting in relation to the 19th century. It contains a clear account of the Norman Earls and has an interesting chapter on 'Work and Play in the Middle Ages'.

A number of papers in the *Transactions of the Leicestershire Archaeological Society* throw a light on medieval life in Leicestershire if not in Leicester itself and perhaps special mention should be made of the articles on 'The Leicestershire Country Parson in the Sixteenth Century' and 'The Leicestershire Farmer in the Sixteenth Century', by Dr. W. G. Hoskins (Vols. XXI and XXII). These, and a number of other important essays by Dr. (now Professor) W. G. Hoskins have been re-issued in book form, as *Essays in Leicestershire History* (Liverpool, 1950).

MEDIEVAL PERIOD

DATES FOR REFERENCE

Kings of England	*Lords and Earls of Leicester*	*Leicester Town*
A.D.	A.D.	A.D.
1066 William the Conqueror	Hugh de Grantmesnil	
		1086 Domesday Survey
1087 William Rufus		
	1094 Ivo de Grantmesnil	
1100 Henry I		
		1101 Leicester plundered
	1107 Robert de Meulan	1107 St. Mary de Castro built (Portmanmota and Gild Merchants are recorded soon after this as being established)

49

Kings of England A.D.	Lords and Earls of Leicester A.D.	Leicester Town A.D.
	1118 Robert le Bossu	
1135 Stephen		
		1143 Abbey of St. Mary de Pratis (consecration)
1154 Henry II		
	1168 Robert Blanchesmains	
		1173 Sack of Leicester
1189 Richard I		
	1190 Robert FitzParnel	
1199 John		
	1204 Simon de Montfort the older (Estates in keeping of Earl of Chester)	1201 Meeting of Barons opposing King John
1216 Henry III		
		(About) 1220 Black Friars
		(About) 1225 Grey Friars
	1231 Simon the younger confirmed in estates	
		1255 Law of Borough English rescinded Jews expelled from Leicester
	1265 Edmund Crouchback (of Lancaster)	
1272 Edward I		
		1295 First burgesses sent to Parliament
	1296 Thomas Earl of Lancaster	
1307 Edward II		
	1322 Henry (of Grosmont) Earl of Lancaster	
1327 Edward III		
		1331 Hospital in Newarke founded
		1340 Epidemic of Pestilence
		1343 Corpus Christi Gild founded
	1345 Henry Duke of Lancaster	
		1348 Black Death
		1355 Collegiate Church in Newarke founded
		1361 Black Death
	1362 John of Gaunt	
1377 Richard II		
1399 Henry IV	1399 Earldom absorbed in Crown	
1413 Henry V		

Kings of England A.D.	Lords and Earls of Leicester A.D.	Leicester Town A.D.
		1414 Parliament in Leicester
1422 Henry VI		
		1426 Parliament (of Bats) 1450 Parliament
1461 Edward IV 1483 Edward V Richard III		
		1485 Richard III sleeps at 'Blue Boar'

Section II

MEDIEVAL BUILDINGS AND STREETS

THE CASTLE, ST. MARY'S, AND THE NEWARKE. There may have been some sort of central barrack building in the fortified Danish town of Leicester, but if so it has left no trace. The Castle that we know was the creation of the Normans and consisted in its earliest form of a steep earth mound surmounted by a wooden structure and a bank and ditch enclosing a bailey to the north-east of this.

The mound, which was probably raised as early as 1068, can be best seen from the river bridge. It was originally much higher—it was levelled down so that a bowling-green could be made on top of it. The enclosed area round the Castle was much larger than the present courtyard. It extended over a large part of Castle Gardens (where some of the foundations of its walls are now exposed) and beyond Castle Street.

The Hall, the principal and earliest surviving building, was built of Dane Hills stone by Robert le Bossu about 1150. Since the time of the first Lancastrian Earl, Edmund Crouchback (1265-96) it was long used for the assizes and now houses the Crown Court; the present-day arrangements for this purpose, as well as the early eighteenth-century brick front, largely conceal its original structure. This can nevertheless be traced and the hall is well worth inspecting. Unfortunately the building is no longer open to visitors at regular hours, due to the frequency of Court sittings. The visitor may see the interior of the Castle Hall only by attending the court proceedings.

Of the much more extensive range of buildings in use during the later Middle Ages there only remain the cellars of the kitchen block, to the south of the Hall, and two gatehouses. One, the turret gateway leading to the Newarke, is in ruins; the other, by the entrance to St. Mary's Church, is still an inhabited house with a room built over the gateway itself. Both these gatehouses date from the fifteenth century.

The Church of St. Mary de Castro was founded at about the time the Castle was built and it originally served as the Castle chapel. At about the time the Castle Hall was built, the church was enlarged and made into a collegiate foundation, served by a dean and canons. The chancel

51

contains a very fine set of late Norman *sedilia*. It is the nave of this Norman building that one enters by the north door and the successive additions and enlargements made in later years provide a fascinating archaeological study. The clue to the principal addition, the great south aisle, is the fact that St. Mary's was really a double church, one half collegiate and the other parochial, the Dean of the college serving also as vicar of the parish. The south aisle, the exclusively parochial portion, had actually a separate dedication, to the Trinity. The Church is kept locked most of the time, but is open on most Saturday and Bank Holiday afternoons from Easter to October, 2 p.m.—5.30 p.m., or at other times by arrangement with the vicar.

The Newarke, now a thoroughfare for traffic, was, when it was built and for long after, a walled close, connected with the Castle by the turret gateway but completely separate from the town. Its principal entrance, the present Magazine Gateway with its large and small arches, led into the road to Aylestone, well outside the South Gates which closed the old High Street between the ends of Millstone Lane and Friar Lane. Inside the Newarke close, Henry Earl of Lancaster and his son, the first Duke (about 1350) built the collegiate church of St. Mary (of the Annunciation) and a hospital for old people which later became the Trinity Hospital. Of the church nothing remains except some arches which are still visible in the basement of the Hawthorn Building of the Polytechnic, and may be viewed by prior application to the Chief Administrative Officer. The hospital has been twice rebuilt but the chapel (which can be seen on application to the matron) retains much of its original form and contains some interesting effigies and medieval relics.

William Wyggeston founded a chantry in the Newarke church and built a house for the priests who served it. This still stands and bears his arms, having survived not only the Reformation and the siege but also a near-miss from a German bomb in 1940. The inside has been much altered, but what remains is used as a part of the Newarke Houses Museum, containing antiquities of local origin. Another medieval building in the Newarke, the former St. Mary's Vicarage, has had to be pulled down in recent years, as it had gone beyond useful repair, but the front wall, up to the first floor level, remains visible as part of the factory entrance and gateway opposite Trinity Hospital.

ST. NICHOLAS', ALL SAINTS', AND ST. MARTIN'S CHURCHES. All Saints' and St. Martin's as well as St. Nicholas' (which as already mentioned has surviving Saxon work) are known to have been in existence directly after the Conquest.

The only distinctive Norman work now visible in All Saints' is the west door but this church, like St. Nicholas', shows interestingly enough how later builders made successive additions to an earlier church by throwing out aisles or a chancel from an existing nave which continued in use.

St. Martin's, on the other hand, is an example of a more drastic reconstruction and enlargement undertaken in the nineteenth century, and except for the interior of the timbered North Porch, this church is now more interesting for its Tudor and later monuments than for surviving traces of its medieval history.

ST. MARGARET'S CHURCH. Contemporary with the parish churches of the town and itself a parish church, St. Margaret's was in a special position. It was in a suburb that owed feudal allegiance to the Bishop of Lincoln and was a prebendal church of Lincoln Cathedral which still has a stall for the Prebend of St. Margaret's, Leicester. Architecturally, the church, which is large and of notably fine proportions, is mainly of two periods, thirteenth and fifteenth century, the tower being part of the later additions. Nineteenth-century restoration has been rather heavy-handed in places. Some twelfth-century work survives, however, and parts of the foundations of the still earlier cruciform church have recently been uncovered.

There is a very fine recumbent effigy of John Penny, Abbot of Leicester Abbey and afterwards Bishop, first of Bangor and then of Carlisle, near the altar against the north wall.

THE ABBEY. The Abbey of St. Mary of the Meadows lay outside the medieval town, to the north of the suburb of St. Margaret's. Founded in 1143 by Robert le Bossu for canons of the Order of St. Augustine, it was rich and important throughout the Middle Ages, but was utterly demolished at the dissolution of the monasteries, very soon after it had received the dying Wolsey and buried his remains. The site came into the possession of the Earl of Huntingdon who built a mansion there, but this house (then owned by the Cavendish family) was burnt down in the Civil War and only a few ruins of it remain.

The Abbey site, which adjoins the Abbey park, is now laid out for the public and the outlines of its church and some of the surrounding buildings, as conjecturally restored, are marked out in stone. Some original work can be seen in the north gateway and in the boundary walls. The brick wall bounding Abbey Lane is traditionally known as Abbot Penny's Wall and the initials J.P. are said to be decipherable amongst other decorations worked in blue brick on its face.

THE GUILDHALL. The Guildhall, originally the hall of the Corpus Christi Gild, was in use during the later Middle Ages but it was so much altered after it became the Town Hall that the present building must be considered as a Tudor rather than a medieval structure, and it will accordingly be more fully noticed among the Tudor buildings of Leicester.

Medieval Streets

The medieval walls of Leicester bounded three sides of a parallelogram, the fourth side, on the West, being the line of the River Soar.

Outside the walls but not far beyond the outer edge of the Town Ditch, ran Soar Lane, The Skeyth or Senvy Gate, Church Gate, Gallowtree Gate (this was a little farther from the wall), Horse Fair Lane and Millstone Lane. Right through the town from the North Gates, near the west end of Senvy Gate to the South Gates near the west end of Mill-stone Lane, ran the High Street. From the West Bridge, Apple Gate and Hot Gate curved up to the High Cross, the centre of the medieval town, across the High Street the Swinemarket continued to the East Gates, debouching into the junction of Church Gate and Gallowtree Gate.

All these streets have been widened out of recognition but they still retain their lines and most of them their names, though Hot Gate is now part of St. Nicholas Circle; the old High Street is Southgate Street and Highcross Street; and the Swinemarket, High Street. Apple Gate was subsequently wrongly labelled Applegate Street; the suffix 'gate' represents an Old Norse and Swedish word 'gata', a road. The High Street was almost the only medieval street that was *called* a street and this may have implied that it was paved; the others, if they led anywhere in particular were generally called Gates, if they did not they were called Lanes.

Some of the meanings of the old street names are self-explanatory: others are too obscure for conjecture. It is reasonably certain, however, that Bond Street (or Parchment Lane) was where the parchment-makers congregated and that Bakehouse Lane was the site of the public bakeries which belonged to the Earl and at which all baking of bread for sale had to be done.

Gallowtree Gate probably meant just what it said: there was a gallows at the top of London Road Hill.

Sanvey Gate has been derived from *Sancta via,* the name being explained by the custom of taking offerings to St. Margaret's church. This guess is hardly supported by one early form, Senvey Gate (1392), though there must have been some medieval reason for adopting this alternative name to the old Danish one, Skeyth, which survived alongside it at least till the late fifteenth century and which probably meant a racecourse. Wood Gate, beyond the North Bridge, was the way by which wood from Leicester Forest was brought into the town.

Cank Street was named after a public well, called The Cank, which stood there. (No one knows why the well was called 'The Cank'. There is however, a dialect word 'to cank', recorded from Leicestershire, meaning 'to gossip'.)

Loseby Lane appears to have been so called since the thirteenth or fourteenth century and may commemorate Henry of Loseby who held land in St. Martin's parish about 1300.

Some names commemorating vanished medieval buildings are worth noting. Grey Friars and Friar Lane are on or near the site of the Franciscan Friary. (A small piece of medieval walling remains in the car park adjoining New Street, and may be connected with the Friary.)

Friars' Causeway (medieval) and Blackfriars Street (modern) commemorate another community, the Dominican or Black Friars sometimes called the Friars Preachers whose house stood not far from the site of the Great Central Station.

A third community, the Austin Friars, had a small canonry between the two arms of the river by the West Bridge and are remembered in the name of St. Augustine Street. This site was excavated in 1975/76.

St. Peter's Lane, between Highcross Street and West Bond Street runs by the site of the church of that name which was pulled down in the sixteenth century and provided the material for building the Free Grammar School.

Blue Boar Lane, the site of which is adjacent to Highcross Street, is where the Blue Boar Inn stood, in which Richard III slept his last night before Bosworth Field. Mill Lane led to the Castle Mill.

FURTHER INFORMATION

A full and clear account of *Leicester Abbey by* Dr. Levi Fox is obtainable from the Information Bureau. His account of *Leicester Castle* is, at the time of writing, out of print. The best general description of Leicester's medieval topography and in particular of its streets is in *Mediæval Leicester*, by C. J. Billson, published by Edgar Backus, Cank Street, Leicester, in 1920. A careful, interesting, and full, though in parts controversial, history and description of *St. Margaret's Church*, by Ernest Morris, F.R.Hist.S., F.R.G.S., may also be obtained from the Church.

Mr. S. H. Skillington's *History of the Trinity Hospital*, though not a topographical work is authoritative and supplies a valuable historical background, and the same author's pamphlet *The Newarke, its Origin and Associations*, though out of print is available in the Reference Library and may be consulted with profit.

The architecture of the Leicester churches is described and discussed in the following contributions to the *Leicestershire Archaeological Society's Transactions:*

'St. Nicholas's Church', Vol. IX, a paper read before the British Archaeological Congress at Leicester, 1900, by Charles Lynam, F.S.A.

'St. Margaret's Church', Vol. II by W. Jackson, 1861.

'St. Martin's Church', Vol. II, by E. Roberts, F.S.A., 1862.

The churches of Leicester were described (Vol. I) by G. A. Poole, M.A., in 1854, and there are shorter accounts of the churches and of other medieval buildings in the reports of the summer meeting 1874 (Vol. IV) and of the annual excursion 1916 (Vol. XI).

The Thirty-Second Annual Report of the Leicester and Leicestershire Society of Architects (1904-5) contains plans and elevations of St. Nicholas' Church previous to the restoration of the Tower.

Section III

(a) REPORT TO SIMON DE MONTFORT
(1253)

[THIS document is No. XX in Records of the Borough of Leicester, 1103-1327 edited by Miss E. M. Bateson. The original is in medieval

Latin and the translation is Miss Bateson's. Trial by Battle (which was normally, but not always, conducted through the medium of hired pugilists) was the Norman substitute for the Saxon Trial by Ordeal, but it is quite possible that in the Danelaw the custom had been a more rational method than either—some sort of trial by Jury. The witnesses in 1253 deposed that in Robert of Meulan's time (that is to say, a century and a quarter before) the men of Leicester had objected to the new procedure, rioted and made a bargain with the Earl which they described. There is no reason to doubt that their story embodies a real tradition but they were, of course, trying to substantiate a case and may not have been above fabricating corroborative details to add verisimilitude to the less convincing parts of their narrative. The list of Jurats shows surnames in the process of crystallization. Professor Hoskins points out that Gamel is a Danish personal name which has become the common Leicestershire surname Gamble.]

The Inquest made by the Jurats underwritten, to wit William of St Lo, Willard of Lincoln, William Baldwin, Alexander Debonair, Jacob Motun, William Gamel, William Hod, Pater Palmer, Nicholas the Burgess, Robert Drury, William Loveman, William Ball, Henry Richard's son, Ralph Fode, William the Chapman, and Thomas Geram about the pence which are called Gavelpence and about Pontage, how and why they were first given and taken. They say on their oath that in the time of Robert of Meulan, then Earl of Leicester, it happened that two kinsmen, to wit Nicholas Hakon's son and Geoffrey Nicholas's son of Leicester, waged a trial by battle for a certain land, about which a plea had arisen between them, and they fought from the hour of Prime to the hour of Noon, and longer, and so fighting with each other, one of them drove the other as far as a certain little ditch, and as the other stood over the little ditch and was about to fall into it, his kinsman said to him, 'Mind you don't fall into the ditch behind you', and immediately there arose such a clamour and such a tumult among the spectators standing and sitting around, that the Lord Earl heard their noise even in the castle, and then asked some people what the noise was, and he was told that two kinsmen were fighting about a piece of land and one of them drove the other as far as a certain little ditch, and as he stood over the ditch and was about to fall into it, the other warned him. The burgesses then moved by pity agreed with the Lord Earl that they would give him 3*d*. a year from each house which had a gable looking on to the high street, on condition that he would grant that all pleas touching them should henceforth be treated and determined by 24 Jurats who were appointed in Leicester of old time; and this was granted to them by the Lord Earl and thus first were raised the pence which are called Gavelpence. After the death of this Earl Robert, Robert his son and heir succeeded, who for the health of his father's soul entirely remitted the aforesaid pence which are called Gavelpence and by his charter gave a quitclaim for ever. The aforesaid charter, with many other writings and charters, was put in the keeping of a certain burgess and clerk who was called Lambert, against whom evil-doers arose in the night, because he was thought to be rich, and they burned his houses and even his feet (!)[1] together with the aforesaid charter and many other writings. Some time after, there was a certain clerk in this town of Leicester by name Simon Maudit, who, for some time after the death of the aforesaid Robert Earl of Leicester who made the charter of quitclaim, had the reeveship of Leicester in farm, and collected and exacted the said pence called Gavel-pence by force and at his own will, distraining all who refused to pay, bidding them shew him a warranty of quitclaim, for he knew very well that the quitclaim was burnt, and so they are paid to this very day.

This inquest was made in the presence of Roger of Ecton then bailiff, Peter Roger's son then mayor of Leicester, Ralph Oliver, Richard of Campeden, and many others on Monday next after the feast of St. Gregory, in the 37th year of the reign of King Henry, son of King John.

The Inquest made by the same Jurats in the presence of the said Roger and Peter and others about the Pontage of Leicester.

They say on their oath that, in the time of the same Earl Robert, the forest of Leicester was so great, thick and full, that it was scarcely possible to go by the paths of that forest, on account of the quantity of dead wood and of boughs blown down by the wind, and then by the will and consent of the Lord Earl and of his Council, it was allowed to those who wished to look for dead wood to have six cart-loads for $1d.$ and a horse-load a week for $\frac{1}{2}d.$ and a man's load a week for $\frac{1}{4}d.$ and these moneys were collected first at the exit of the wood, afterwards outside the town of Leicester nearer to the wood, and then these moneys were collected at the bridges of the town of Leicester, where at first there was a certain keeper called Penkrich, to whom the Lord Earl at his request afterwards granted a certain space near the bridge on which to build, that there he might collect the custom more conveniently. And this Penkrich for some time after collected the said moneys both for green wood and felled wood which (custom) used to be paid for dead wood, and so afterwards it passed into a custom. And that the truth of this inquest may appear the more clearly and be the more obvious, it can well be perceived by the fact that strangers from whatever part they may have come, carrying wood or timber, whether it be from the forest of Arden or from Cannock Chase or from Needwood forest, or who-ever they might be, pay no pontage, nor ever used to pay it, those only excepted who came from Leicester forest.

[1] ?The feet of the indented records. Cf. Pollock and Maitland, ii, 97.—Miss Bateson's note.

(b) THE BOOK OF MARGERY KEMPE
(1436)

A modern version by W. Butler-Bowdon

(Jonathan Cape, 30 Bedford Square, London, 1936)

[The autobiography, lost for several centuries, has recently been re-discovered; not the original MS. but an early copy. Previously only a few extracts were known. A literal transcript of the MS. has been published by the Early English Text Society.

Margery Kempe was a religious enthusiast who was just not venerated as a saint, just not burnt as a heretic and just not shut up as a lunatic. The reader of her autobiography will probably conclude that on the whole, her contemporaries dealt with this oddity more sensibly than earlier and more sympathetically than later ages would have done.

The extracts given below are chosen to show, in particular, the variety of jurisdiction which existed in Leicester in the fifteenth century. Margery Kempe was ingenious and successful in playing off the ecclesiastical against the lay authorities—on one side the Bishop of Lincoln, the Abbot, and the Dean (probably the Dean of St. Mary's of the Newarke) and on the other the Earl's Steward and the Mayor. Her account of her visit to Leicester makes, as a whole, a fascinating short story. The whole book gives an illuminating picture of medieval ways of life.]

Ch. 46

So she and the good man, Thomas Marchale went forth and took her hostel and there ate their meat. When they had eaten, she prayed Thomas Marchale to write a letter and send it to her husband, that he might fetch her home. And while the letter was in writing, the hosteler came up to her chamber in great haste, and took away her scrip and bade her come quickly and speak with the Mayor. And so she did.

Then the Mayor asked her of what country she was, and whose daughter she was.

'Sir', she said, ' I am of Lynne in Norfolk, a good man's daughter of the same Lynne, who hath been mayor five times of that worshipful borough, and alderman also many years; and I have a good man, also a burgess of the said town of Lynne, for my husband'.

'Ah!' said the Mayor, 'Saint Katherine told what kindred she came of, and yet ye are not like her, for thou art a false strumpet, a false lollard, and a false deceiver of the people, and I shall have thee in prison'.

And she answered: 'I am as ready, sir, to go to prison for God's love, as ye are ready to go to church'.

When the Mayor had long chidden her and said many evil and horrible words to her, and she, by the grace of Jesus, had reasonably answered to all that he could say, he commanded the jailer's man to lead her to prison.

The jailer's man, having compassion on her with weeping tears, said to the Mayor:

'Sir, I have no house to put her in unless I put her amongst men'.

Then she was moved with compassion for the man who had compassion on her. Praying for grace and mercy to that man, as for her own soul, she said to the Mayor:

'I pray you, sir, put me not among men, that I may keep my chastity, and my bond of wedlock to my husband, as I am bound to do'.

Then said the jailer his own self to the Mayor: 'Sir, I will be under bond to keep this woman in safe ward till ye will have her back'.

Then there was a man of Boston who said to the good wife, where she was at hostel:

'Forsooth', he said, 'in Boston this woman is held to be a holy woman and a blessed woman'.

Then the jailer took her into his ward, and led her home into his own house, and put her in a fair chamber, shutting the door with a key, and commanding his wife the key to keep.

Nevertheless he let her go to church when she would, and let her eat at his own table and made her right good cheer for Our Lord's sake, thanked be Almighty God thereof.

Ch. 47

Then the steward of Leicester, a seemly man, sent for the said creature to the jailer's wife, and she—for her husband was not at home —would not let her go to any man, steward or otherwise. When the jailer knew thereof he came himself, and brought her before the steward. The steward anon, as he saw her, spake Latin unto her, many priests standing about to hear what she would say. She said to the steward:

'Speak English if ye please, for I understand not what ye say'.

The steward said to her:

'Thou liest falsely, in plain English'.

Then she said to him again:

'Sir, ask what question ye will in English, and by the grace of My Lord Jesus Christ I will answer you reasonably thereto'.

Then asked he many questions, to which she answered so readily and reasonably that he could get no cause against her.

.   .   .   .   .   .

Ch. 48

On a Wednesday, the said creature was brought into a church of All Hallows[1] in Leicester, in which place, before the High Altar, was set the Abbot of Leicester with some of his canons, the Dean of Leicester a

---

[1] All Saints'.

worthy clerk. There were also many friars and priests; also the Mayor of the same town with many others of the lay people. There were so many people that they stood on stools to behold her and wonder at her.

The said creature lay on her knees, making her prayers to Almighty God, that she might have grace, wit, and wisdom, so to answer that day as might be most pleasure and worship to Him, most profit to her soul, and best example to the people.

Then there came a priest to her, and took her by the hand and brought her before the Abbot and his assessors sitting at the Altar, who made her swear on a book that she should answer truly to the Articles of Faith, as she felt in them.

And first they explained the Blissful Sacrament of the Altar, charging her to say right as she believed therein. Then she said:

'Sirs, I believe in the Sacrament of the Altar in this wise; that whatever man hath taken the order of priesthood, be he ever so vicious a man in his living, if he duly say those words over the bread, that our Lord Jesus Christ said when He made His Maundy among His disciples, where He sat at the supper, I believe that it is His very Flesh and His Blood, and no material bread; and never may it be unsaid, be it once said'.

And so she answered forth to all the Articles, as many as they would ask her, so that they were well pleased.

The Mayor, who was her deadly enemy, said: 'In faith, she meaneth not in her heart what she sayeth with her mouth'.

And the clerks said to him: 'Sir, she answereth right well to us'.

Then the Mayor strongly rebuked her and said many reprehensible words and ungoodly, which are more expedient to be concealed than expressed.

· · · · · ·

Then the Mayor said to her 'I will know why thou go-est in white clothes, for I trow thou art come hither to have away our wives from us, and lead them with thee'.

'Sir', she said, 'ye shall not know from my mouth, why I go in white clothes; ye are not worthy to know it. But Sir, I will tell it to these worthy clerks, with good will in the manner of confession. Ask them if they will tell it to you!'

Then the clerks prayed the Mayor to go down from them with the other people. And when they were gone, she knelt on her knees before the Abbot, and the Dean of Leicester and a Preaching Friar, a worshipful clerk, and told these three clerks how Our Lord, by revelation, warned her and bade her wear white clothes, ere she came to Jerusalem.

'And so I have told my ghostly fathers. And therefore they have charged me that I should go thus, for they dare not act against my feelings, for dread of God; and if they durst, they would, full gladly. Therefore, sirs, if the Mayor will learn why I go in white, ye may say, if ye like, that my ghostly fathers bid me go so; and then shall ye tell no lies, and he shall not know the truth'.

So the clerks called up the Mayor again, and told him in council that her ghostly fathers had charged her to wear white clothes, and she had bound herself to their obedience.

Then the Mayor called her to him, saying: 'I will not let thee go for anything that thou canst say, unless thou wilt go to my lord of Lincoln for a letter, inasmuch as thou art in his jurisdiction, saying that I may be discharged of thee'.

She said: 'I dare speak to my lord of Lincoln right well, for, I have had of him right good cheer before this time'.

Then other men asked her if she were in charity with the Mayor, and she said 'Yea and with all creatures'.

Then she, bowing to the Mayor, prayed him to be in charity with her, with weeping tears, and forgive her anything in which she had displeased him.

And he gave her goodly words for a while, so that she thought all was well, and he was her good friend, but afterwards she knew well it was not so.

And thus she had leave of the Mayor to go to my lord of Lincoln, and fetch a letter by which the Mayor should be excused.

PART III

TUDOR AND STUART LEICESTER

THE NEWARKE HOUSES: AN EARLY RENAISSANCE BUILDING OF THE ELIZABETHAN-JACOBEAN PERIOD

BELGRAVE HOUSE, EIGHTEENTH CENTURY: A LATER RENAISSANCE BUILDING IN THE
CLASSICAL TRADITION WHICH FOLLOWED THE CIVIL WAR

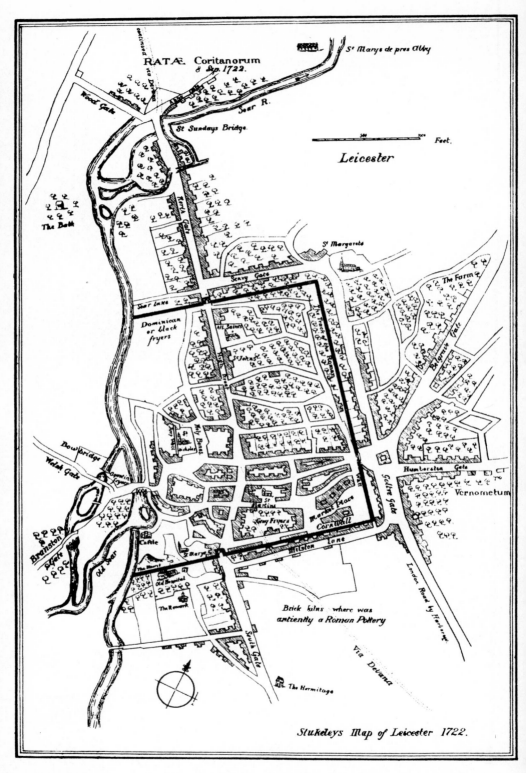

EIGHTEENTH-CENTURY LEICESTER. COMPARE WITH MEDIEVAL LEICESTER, FACING PAGE 37 AND
NINETEENTH-CENTURY LEICESTER BETWEEN PLATES AT PAGES 120-121 AND 138-139

Section I

TUDOR AND STUART LEICESTER

THE Tudor Age was, for England, a time of great and new opportunities which were grasped with both hands. For the inland corporate towns, of which Leicester was typical, it was an age of disappointment, frustration, and actual decay. It had seemed at one time as though, when the feudal structure disintegrated, such towns might become, like some of the continental cities, independent economic units, city-states, trading and making treaties with one another; in the last resort making war on one another. The strong central government of the Tudor monarchs put an end to that dream and, once and for all, subordinated the economic and political interests of municipalities to those of the nation.

It was, as we can see now, the only way for England to survive, for the conditions under which the inland towns had been its mainstay were passing away. For fifteen hundred years, in Leicestershire and elsewhere, men had been cutting down, but not planting, trees. For a thousand years they had been using, but not repairing, the Roman roads. For five hundred years they had been sending a steady drain of coined gold and silver out of the country towards the East in payment for silks and spices. They had been living on capital and their capital was coming to an end. Certainly they had built up other capital assets; they could point to many fine buildings and to a fertile countryside, but the buildings and much of the land had been handed over to a Church which many people were ceasing to regard as a national asset. The new opportunities, the new sources of capital and income that were to set right the national balance sheet, came from the opening of sea roads, international trade, the exploitation of the New World, and, at home, the fuller economic exploitation of the countryside in the new sheep-farming. Seaports prospered, London grew enormously; the country gentlemen, or those who took the occasion to become country gentlemen, wrested first the Church lands and then the government of the country from necessitous monarchs. For the corporate towns there were, in this age, no new opportunities. They fought hard to hold and increase their privileges but on balance they lost more than they gained. If nothing happened to turn the tide—and to many of them nothing did happen—their corporate status would become first an anomaly, then a political scandal and at last only a quaint tradition.

Something did happen to turn the tide in Leicester, but it had hardly begun to have effect before the reign of the last Stuart. The period as a whole is one in which the importance and prosperity of Leicester as a town declined in relation to some other towns and to the country as a whole, although at the same time the standard of living of many, perhaps most, individuals was steadily rising. This is the background against which the series of dramatic or memorable events that for most of us make up the substance of English history was seen from the streets and houses of Leicester.

For a generation after Bosworth Field, the surface of life was smooth. Ideas, spread by the new printing press, were stirring but they had not yet found vent in action. The wise parsimony of Henry VII established a firm central organisation of government without laying intolerable burdens on the towns which were the chief contributors to his exchequer. After the wars were done, peaceable men breathed more freely, though roving bands of discharged soldiers and of peasants dispossessed by the continuing enclosures were a constant source of anxiety, expense, and sometimes danger.

Leicestershire was a considerable sheep-farming and wool-producing area, but the manufacture of woollen cloth, which England was beginning to recapture from Flanders, in the main passed Leicester by. For the weaving of broadcloth two things were required—a short wool and ample water power for the operation of fulling. Leicester had neither. The long wool of the local breed of sheep was very suitable for making worsted cloth but for some reason that is not so clear this manufacture centred in the villages of East Anglia where domestic factories were developed on an important scale. Perhaps it was found simpler in view of the hazards and difficulties of road transport, to take the raw wool, rather than finished cloth, from the Midlands to somewhere nearer to the seaboard. Apart from knitting articles for local requirements, Leicester's connection with the wool trade seems to have been mainly as a warehousing centre.

A few citizens grew rich. William Wyggeston was twice Mayor of Leicester but he made his money as a wool merchant of the Staple of Calais, England's outpost on the Continent. Like good men before him, he founded a chantry where priests would pray for his soul. A few years later, in 1513, unconsciously or consciously falling in line with newer and more material ideas of benefaction, he founded a hospital for old people. Luckily for later ages and for his memory he endowed it, not with a fixed income, but with certain actual lands. As some of these were in the coal-bearing area of Leicestershire and others have become available for building purposes, the income of the charity has enormously risen so that Wyggeston's benefaction has extended far beyond his original conception. But even if all his lands had remained agricultural, his bequest would have avoided the effects of depreciation of money values which had already begun and which has maintained its trend ever since. We see, by contrast, how sadly John Whatton failed to match the means to the intention when, in 1653, he left 2s. 6d. weekly to maintain a poor widow in Wyggeston's Hospital, together with 10s. a year, half of which was for the Master of the Hospital 'to desire his countenance for the said poor widow, that she be not wronged' and the other half for the Mayor and Justices 'to drink in wine together'.

William Wyggeston and a few others were exceptions. Most of the burgesses of Leicester were either retail traders or working craftsmen labouring in their own homes beside their apprentices; and small tradesmen in a not very prosperous town were in a poor position to stand up for their rights against a Tudor monarch: they badly needed a friend at court.

For many generations they found a good one in the representative for the time being of a newly powerful local family. From the time of Henry VIII until the Civil War 'The Earl' was a potent factor in Leicester affairs but he was not the Earl of Leicester; he was the Earl of Huntingdon, the head of the Hastings family and lord of the Castle of Ashby-de-la-Zouch. Usually the Earl or a member of his family was also Lord Lieutenant of Leicestershire and Steward of the Honor of Leicester—the Honor being a widespread group of lands owing fees to the old Earldom of Leicester, now absorbed in the Crown.

The Earl considered it his prerogative to nominate the men (not always natives of Leicestershire) who should be sworn as freemen so that they could represent the town in Parliament, he supervised and assisted measures for the relief of the poor and he led the soldiers levied locally for national defence. (There was an instruction to the Corporation in 1589 that these must in future be furnished in stated proportions with muskets, calivers and corslets with pikes and that *all the bows and arrows and bills generally must be refused*.) The third Earl of Huntingdon, in addition to his seat in Ashby, set up a mansion, which he enlarged, at the side of the (present) High Street. This came to be known as the Lord's Place and the last fragment of it, the Huntingdon Tower, was only pulled down when the street was widened, about 1900. He and his successors considered themselves very much *in loco parentis* to the burgesses. On the very rare occasions when the townsmen ventured to disobey their patron, their explanations of the 'mistake' were in the very best preparatory school tradition of unconvincing ingenuity. Once, a Mr. Belgrave, whom the Earl particularly disliked, was elected to Parliament. They said that he came in a *blue coat* (the Hastings colour) and that they assumed, or were given to understand, that he had suddenly become 'the Earl's man'. On another occasion, a gibbet, which the Earl had put up to overawe countrymen who were threatening revolt, was mysteriously taken down and chopped up—by children, said the Mayor. 'I rather think', wrote the Earl, 'that some greater power than children have done it, and very likely through your remissness; but the certainty hereof I hope hereafter to be informed of'.

This, however, was in James I's reign when even burgesses were just beginning to question authority. A hundred years earlier, the only question—and it was not one for burgesses—had been whether supreme power should rest with the king or with the pope. That issue was, as it happened, settled at Leicester where Wolsey died, full of pious speeches but persistently evading the inquiry as to what he had done with a certain sum of fifteen hundred pounds—the inquiry might have been made far wider if there had been time. 'Well, well, Master Kingston', quoth he, 'I see the matter against me, how it is framed; but if I had served God as diligently as I have done the king, he would not have given me over in my grey hairs'.

Wolsey was a bureaucrat of genius and possibly the significance of the last sentence lay in the fact that by allowing the new class of learned laymen to establish a hold on his organization he had provided the king with a tool which he could use against the Church. However that may be, bureaucrats of any kind are seldom regarded with either loyalty or affection by those whom they tax and control: it was probably not with any deep emotion that the Mayor of Leicester, sent for officially, viewed the body lying in Leicester Abbey. Certainly the people of Leicester took no trouble, when the Abbey itself lay in ruins a few years later, to preserve even the memory of the site of Wolsey's tomb. That was a pity, but it is only fair to remember that in 1539 a too-marked interest in Wolsey's resting-place — or, for that matter, in the resting-place of Richard III—might have been construed by the authorities as something less laudable and more dangerous than solicitude for future antiquarians and sightseers.

The Abbey and the Friaries fell together. A scheme appears to have been drafted under which, out of the Church's revenues, thirteen new bishoprics were to be endowed. Leicester would have been one of them and in this case the abbey church, like that of Peterborough, would no doubt have survived as its cathedral. But the royal need for money was too great, the new sees were reduced to six, and Leicester remained in the diocese of Lincoln.[1]

A few years later the Chantries were also suppressed and the properties that endowed them were leased to various people by the Crown. In this case, after a long interval, the Corporation itself got a chance to gain some advantage from royal necessity. In 1587, pleading the general poverty of the town and the decay of these houses in particular, they represented that 'Her Majesty hath no timber near in these parts to repair the houses, and the tenants are so poor that they cannot repair them; so that in the end all will decay, and her Majesty's rents be lost'. They added, perhaps quite truly, that 'It is a pity to behold the great gaps and ruins—yea even in the principal streets of this town' but certainly quite untruly, 'thirty parish churches there come to six, and four and twenty wards to ten'. What they did not say was that in about

[1] Till 1839 when it was transferred to Peterborough. Leicester became a separate diocese in 1926 for the first time since 874.

fifteen years' time most of the leases would fall in so that the properties could be let at advanced rents to wealthier tenants or on easy terms to the Corporation's own members. Whether the Crown's agents knew this or not, Elizabeth, with the Armada almost in sight, was willing to hand over the properties and to give the Corporation the right to buy and sell land, together with the profits of the weekday shambles, for the substantial annual rent of £137 13s. 7d.—equivalent to rather more than £13,800 at 1976 values. It is this transaction—the long delayed establishment of the right of fee-farm—that constitutes Leicester's first full and formal Charter of Incorporation.

A great deal had happened besides economic changes in the long life-time between the foundation of the latest chantries and their sale as decay-tenements. Edward VI had succeeded Henry VIII and anyone who leaned to the doctrines of Geneva had liberty and encouragement to sell or destroy church ornaments and vestments. Mary had come to the throne, Lady Jane Grey, gentle scholar of Bradgate, had gone to the scaffold, and the vestments had been replaced; it was not so easy to replace stained glass and sculptured saints. A young man of twenty-four went to the stake in Leicester for denying transubstantiation: if the spectators were shocked, it was not because burning was the penalty for heresy but because his views were those privately held by very many respectable people. When Elizabeth succeeded to the throne she wisely burned only people whose views were markedly eccentric or whose expression of them implied a political attitude that might be dangerous to the state. A shoemaker, towards the end of her reign, had a narrow escape when he said that 'within these six years he hoped to see more morrice-dancing than ever he had seen'—a dark saying which might have meant that he hoped for a restoration of Catholic customs under another monarch. Fortunately the judge accepted his explanation that, the puritan mayor having pulled down the maypole, 'he had heard one Mr. Hunter say that when he came to be mayor of Leicester he would allow a morrice, being out of service-time', and that he had merely repeated the speech, 'not meaning any hurt therein'.

The shoemaker was acquitted, but his hopes of more morrice dancing were not fulfilled. Merrie England, merrier no doubt for some classes than for others, was rapidly passing away. The Riding of the George, the appurtenances of which were sold in Edward VI's time, does not seem to have been revived. If there was still a civic procession on Corpus Christi day it had little of its former magnificence. The provision of a town preacher or lecturer was now considered a more appropriate way of giving official recognition to the community's religious needs. In the same spirit, the Corporation, instead of repairing the decaying church of St. Peter, took it down and used the material, or the proceeds of its sale, to build a grammar school. Such schools were being founded in most towns: a much more unusual enterprise was the gradual collection of what must have been one of the very few public libraries in the country.[1]

The general impression one forms of Leicester, as it passed from the Tudor to the Stuart age, is the not unexpected one of a community of hard-headed men, conservatively competent in the management of their own and the town's business, jealous of outsiders, inclined to a puritanism which frowned rather on demonstrative popular gaiety than on solid personal comfort, more accessible to the intellectual aspects of culture than sensitive to aesthetic appeal. William Herrick, whose father and brother were Leicester ironmongers, earned his money and a knighthood in London but came back to live on his newly purchased estate at Beaumanor: he knew that he would be not without honour in his own country. The orphaned nephew to whom Sir William was, in Mr. S. H. Skillington's charitable phrase, 'a frugal guardian', was probably as wise in thinking that for a lyric poet his family's home-town offered less chance of fame and happiness than the university, the court, and a Devonshire vicarage.

Leicester would no doubt have been better off with a poet or two but it would certainly have been much worse off without some hard-headed, well-to-do business-men who could tackle the two pressing and interlinked problems of that time—unemployment and the plague. Every ten years or so a particularly virulent outbreak of the latter cut off communication with London, stopped the fairs and brought even local trade practically to a standstill. On the other hand, during the intervals when plague was not actively killing them off, the poorer classes increased in numbers beyond the town's capacity to provide normal employment. In the first case relief had to be provided for people actually shut up in their houses and forbidden to trade; in the second, some productive work for idle hands had to be sought.

The able-bodied poor were a problem of a new kind because they were now free men with neither the disabilities nor the rights of villeins. No one person was responsible for them and there was no particular bit of land from which they could wring their sustenance or starve. The forest itself, from which they used to carry firewood on their backs, had gone. Charles I enclosed it and, under pressure, made a compensatory 'gift' of 5s. 4d. each to sixty poor householders to buy a load of wood. Other benefactors followed suit with gifts for coals or bread or, in the case of William Ive, 'eight 10s. gowns for eight poor widows dwelling within the borough of Leicester in the first week in clean Lent'.

None of these excellent gifts, however, could be more than palliatives and we must give our Tudor and Stuart forebears full credit for the fact that they did look deeper and face the real problem of preventing as well as relieving chronic poverty. We may smile, it is true, at the paro-

[1] As early as 1587 there seems to have been a library in St. Martin's Church. This was moved to its present home in 1632 when the bulk of the collection that still exists was made. The first public library in London was not established till 1684. (See G. M. Trevelyan, *English Social History*: 'The Later Stuarts.')

chial wisdom of their first resolve to admit no one to Leicester whose family would by any possibility become a charge on the town. When, on one occasion, they tried to exact a bond of £200 from a newcomer against this contingency they were shrewdly told that 'for your corporation or any other towne whatsoever, to provide in future what shall befall in that respect, were very inconvenient, because you and others do now know your present estates, little knowing what may become of posterities'.

Much less ridiculous, though still aimed at exclusiveness, was the attempt to confine retail trade in the borough to freemen, that is to say, to the contemporary equivalent of substantial ratepayers. The corporation argued that these people were being impoverished and therefore made less able to bear either national or local burdens by the competition of goods manufactured in the country or in market towns where the standards of craftsmanship, quality, and wages were lower. In a petition sent in 1540 to the Chancellor of the Duchy of Lancaster on this subject, they did not fail to paint the usual gloomy picture: 'the grater parte of the hye strete of the sayd towne within the sayed XL yerez ys goon to ruyn and decaye'. In this matter the Tudor government did lend a sympathetic ear to the complaints of the corporate towns. A whole series of acts, culminating in the Elizabethan Statute of Artificers attempted with some success to check the drift of industry away from such towns, partly by giving them a preference in the right to take apprentices for certain trades and partly by making the rigorous standard of seven years' apprenticeship universal.

The fact remained, however, that there was an increasing number of people in Leicester who were not freemen, who were not wanted as apprentices, and who had to live somehow. The combination of doles to the workless and a protected standard of living for sheltered industries gave a breathing-space for the present; there was yet another expedient which held promise of a new kind for the future. This was a scheme for advancing capital to someone so that he could 'set the poor on work', the work being usually weaving or the knitting of caps and stockings. Exactly how the system worked out, is not quite clear; knitted caps were not always fashionable and some attempt was made to enforce the wearing of them; at one time the nominated clothier was reported to be 'decayed' (presumably in his finances); there is no evidence that those who were set on work ceased to be poor. Nevertheless, somehow, the idea was emerging that the answer to unemployment in towns was the development of a capitalist structure of industry. It was the answer that was to hold the field without serious dispute for a couple of centuries.

A related idea that still seems a good one to most of us was that of Sir Thomas White, a London merchant who, for some reason, had a warm feeling not only for Coventry where his bequest went initially, but for all the Midland corporate towns. Leicester shared with Nottingham, Northampton, and Warwick, a balance of his benefaction which was, by a deed of gift, to be devoted to lending young men sums of money free of interest to set themselves up in business as minor capitalists. Like William Wyggeston he fortunately gave, not a fixed sum, but the income from certain lands. Partly for this reason, partly because hardly any of the principal lent has been lost, some thousands of pounds are now lent annually in Leicester, to the great benefit of many young citizens.

The Tudor age had seen an economic, a political, and a religious revolution, all without wholesale bloodshed. In the Stuart period, economic change slowed down as if to give scope for the culmination of other struggles. The time was approaching for the town of Leicester to make one more of its brief and unlucky appearances on the stage of English history. As usual, its role pathetically resembled that of Mr. Pickwick between the rival editors.

When the issue was finally joined, Leicester was held for the Parliamentarians. It is probable that, if pressed, a fair working majority of citizens would have voted for that side rather than the other, but it is almost certain that if neutrality had been possible when it came to actual fighting their choice of it would have been nearly unanimous. The gentlemen of the county, the chief holders of power and leaders of opinion were themselves divided. The Earl of Huntingdon's influence was strongly for the King: a younger son, Henry Hastings, afterwards Lord Loughborough, led the royal forces in the county and held Ashby castle. On that side too was the dowager Countess of Devonshire in the big house at the Abbey, on the very threshold of the town. On the other side, however, were the Greys of Bradgate, headed by the Earl of Stamford, and Sir Arthur Hazlerigg of Noseley, one of the 'five members' whose attempted arrest had done so much to precipitate the conflict.

It was only after a good deal of manœuvring that Lord Stamford gained control in Leicester. In July and August 1642 the King himself visited Leicester twice, was received with ceremony, made a speech expressing, not very confidently, his belief in the loyalty of the citizens and attended a civic service in St. Martin's church. Prince Charles, always a realist, graciously accepted 'a fair wrought purse with fifty pieces of gold' from the Corporation.

There was a good deal less graciousness, and on a long view, less political realism about Prince Rupert when, a month later, he made a very peremptory demand for £2,000 and sent six dragoons to fetch it. He got £500 and no doubt did a more than equivalent amount of harm to his cause for although the King promptly disavowed and apologised for the demand, it does not appear that he returned the money.

For three years after that, Leicester maintained a Parliamentary garrison which skirmished in a desultory fashion with parties of Royalists from Ashby and Belvoir. In 1645 the critical time came. The main armies were in the field in the Midlands. Oxford was besieged by the Roundheads and it was with the intention of drawing off their forces as well as of hampering their route to the North that Prince Rupert decided to take Leicester. There is nothing very glorious to tell about the siege except that those who fought, fought hard. Medieval walls were not meant to withstand cannon—in fact, after five hundred years of peace they were not really fit to withstand any determined assault. Suburbs and stray houses sprawled out beyond them giving protection to the attackers. Although earthworks were thrown up and houses thrown down there was not enough time to make the place really defensible. Moreover, until the last moment, preparations for defence were largely left in the hands of the civic authorities whom the soldiers blamed, but whom we shall hardly be inclined to blame, for reluctance to pull down people's houses in preparation for a siege that might never happen.

Rupert may only have been a moderately good general, but a worse one, with the artillery and men at his command, could have made short work of Leicester. Fortunately, he did make short work of it: there was no long heart-breaking siege. For a couple of days he pounded the Newarke Walls, battered a breach in them, and then, when his summons to surrender was refused, sent his troops in to the assault. In a few hours it was all over, though the fighting in the streets was as fierce as on the ramparts. According to one report, King Charles rode up to the High Cross 'clad in bright armour' and, seeing the soldiers maltreating prisoners, said, 'I do not care if they cut them more, for they are mine enemies'.[1] According to another, he repeated, as he watched the battle from the Raw Dykes, 'Dear and loving subjects, cry quarter, dear and loving subjects, obey'. It is not impossible to believe of him that both stories are true.

Leicester was taken on the last day of May. Its capture, a minor point gained for the Royalists, brought on the Battle of Naseby which lost them the game and avenged, though it did not recompense, the citizens of all political complexions who were the chief sufferers. On 14 June the King passed by or through the town again, in full retreat from Naseby. On 12 February the next year, he slept at the 'Angel', a prisoner under guard.

The Corporation of Leicester (but not the Town Clerk who was dismissed for his supposed Royalist sympathies) had the satisfaction of being on the winning side and of receiving £1,500 out of the estates of 'delinquents'. They can have had little other satisfaction. A number of people had been killed, most people had been robbed, some houses had been pulled down, some had been knocked down by cannon shot, some, notably the Countess of Devonshire's mansion, had been carelessly or maliciously burned down. 'The saltpetre man', looking for an essential

---

[1] This speech was quoted at his trial. It is fair to say that he referred almost certainly to the Scots who were among the garrison, and not to the Leicester citizens themselves.

ingredient of gunpowder, had dug up mud floors and pulled down mud walls. All this damage was added to the general 'decay' resulting from poverty and the scarcity of building materials that had been noticeable for so long.

The most immediately depressing feature of the Brave New World was the fact that the Army, besides interfering in matter of religious observance and the appointment of ministers, received many local Crown revenues as their perquisite. The Honor of Leicester was 'pitcht upon by a regiment' and for a time the Corporation protested in vain that some of the dues had been granted to themselves by Charles I and others assigned for the support of the town charities.

Besides settling such troublesome matters, the Mayors and Justices had the difficult task of enforcing, as far as they could, their ideal of a uniform and moderate puritanism in a society that included some back-sliders and a number of intemperate zealots. They fined people for working, or allowing their children to play, on the Lord's day, for playing 'shove-grote', for ringing church bells contrary to the ordinance, for drinking the king's health; they impounded heretical books and committed Quakers[1] to prison.

At the same time the Corporation took thought for the material benefit of the town and the increase of their own powers, approving a scheme (which was not very successful) for bringing water from the Castle Mill to the High Cross and preparing their case for a new charter which would give them full jurisdiction over the suburbs of St. Margaret's and St. Leonard's, the Castle and the Newarke.

When Richard Cromwell succeeded his father, the moment seemed favourable for pressing the latter project, but Richard, Lord Protector, proved to be only Tumble Down Dick; General Monk marched down from Scotland in 1659-60 and very soon the Mayor was assuring the M.P. for the borough of the 'great joy and acclamacions' with which the 'Proclamacion' of King Charles II had been received. ('Sir, this short Accompt I by thadvice of my Brethren thought fitt to give you for your satisfaccion and for the prevencion of any Calumnyes that may be cast on this Burrough'.)

In the same spirit the Corporation welcomed back Lord Lough-borough, and reinstated the Town Clerk whom they had dismissed.

All this show of loyalty may have been sincere, but it was not accepted at its face-value. There were no actual reprisals but no less than forty out of the seventy-two members of the Common Hall were removed and replaced by new men.

---

[1] Quakerism was strong in parts of Leicestershire and George Fox, founder of the Society of Friends, was himself a Leicestershire man. His Journal gives an interesting account of a dispute in St. Martin's Church and also of two occasions on which he suffered arrest in Leicester, once under the Commonwealth and once after the Restoration.

The Restoration, or perhaps the Civil War itself, ended the long era in which the Corporation had been a body fully and worthily representing the town. Its new members may have been politically acceptable but they lacked administrative experience and admitted the fact in so many words on one occasion. Lack of authority and of unanimity as well as a legal decision prevented them resisting the assertion by the freemen of a long disused right to vote at Parliamentary elections. Finally, when Charles II in 1684 obliged them to surrender their charter and accept a new one, the number of councillors was reduced from forty-eight to the more usual number of thirty-six, no extra privileges were granted and the appointments of the chief officials were made subject to confirmation by the Crown.

It is rather curious that the freemen's right to vote was confirmed by this charter. Perhaps the commonalty of Leicester was considered more reliable than even a 'regulated' Corporation. Or possibly the Court party saw their way to influence elections by methods which the Recorder in 1676 had hesitated to recommend to the Mayor: 'As for the expence of a Noble treat to the whole corporacion uppon the election no man will Deny It but to hyre or Ingage votes unduly by Drinking on Any syde is so great A cryme tis not to be suffered'. It was a crime which, I am afraid, was suffered many times in the century and a half that followed.

The history of the Corporation, however, or even the history of the freemen, would no longer be the history of Leicester. The wheel had come full circle and it was not by her retention of privileges but by her failure to retain privileges that the town gained new opportunities to grow and prosper. In 1674 a very significant petition was presented to the Mayor by certain persons interested in the production of knitted hosiery—probably it was still hand-knitted. These people, independent successors of the men who had been employed by the Corporation to set the poor on work, represented that they were doing a new trade which therefore should not be confined to freemen; that if the freemen by employing trained workmen could make better articles and out-sell the petitioners none could hinder them; that if only the best workmen were employed the children could not be taught and the trade would perish; that 'it is not the curious making of a few stockings but the general making of many, that is most to the public good'; that driving the petitioners from town would be much to the damage of the town and hinder about 1,000 poor people of the work they now have; and so on, using arguments that a century earlier would have seemed almost blasphemy and that a century later would have been accepted as almost gospel.

Whether by decision or by default, the Corporation let them have their way. Another period in Leicester's history was coming to an end, not because James II fled the country in 1688, not because George I came over in 1714, but because, towards the end of the seventeenth century, people in towns like Leicester began to think differently and thereafter to live differently. The petitioners of 1674 were the fore-runners of the men whose views dominated economic doctrine and commercial practice for the next two hundred years. Henceforward, they said in effect, prices, wages, the location and the methods of indus-try must be regulated neither by municipalities nor by the state but by the unfettered action of the laws of supply and demand.

It so happens that in some matters the pendulum has swung back again, so that our point of view is nearer to that of the seventeenth century than it was a hundred years ago. How fast and how far men's minds travelled can be measured by the outlook of James Thompson who published his *History of Leicester* in 1849. He notes, as from a position of secure superiority, the attempts to deal with a great scarcity of corn in 1622. 'The lords of the Privy Council issued an order to the large towns of the country, enjoining upon the authorities that, as in times of scarcity barley formed the bread-corn of the people, which was largely consumed in the making of strong ale and beer, the strength of the same should be moderated, so that there should be no vain consumption of the grain of the kingdom'. After describing how, in Leicester, malting was so profitable that even Wyggeston's Hospital was used as a malthouse, how ministers were requested to preach against wholesale buying of barley and how riots were threatened, he adds as his final comment: 'In consequence of these things a great number of restrictions were imposed upon all maltsters and buyers of corn—*such indeed, as would be considered highly absurd at the present period*'.

Some other ideas which were widely entertained under the Tudors and Stuarts, and which may or may not be considered highly absurd at the present period, were going out of fashion at the same time. There was, for instance, the idea that it is better to burn, kill, or imprison one's fellow-countrymen than to allow political and religious uniformity to be disturbed by the promulgation of unorthodox views. And there was the related idea that it is better to be burned, killed, or imprisoned than to yield a political or theological point. Perhaps in Leicester religious toleration was more generally welcomed than in most of the country because in Leicester penal statutes aimed primarily at catholics bore hardly on the large numbers of respectable dissenters.

We can, if we like, say that the end of one period and the beginning of another was heralded in 1680 when the first stocking-frame was set up in the town. Or we can, with equal reason, say that the important date was 1708 when two dissenting bodies, the Independents and the Presby-terians, joined forces to build the Great Meeting-house in brick—a material that had hardly been used in Leicestershire before, except in a few buildings magnificently expressive of privilege, wealth, and power.[1]

[1] Such as Kirby Muxloe Castle, Quenby Hall, and John Penny's 'new brick workes' at the Abbey.

But exact dates and particular events are only significant because they indicate the period and direction of a general change. At about the time that a new century and a new royal line were coming in, stocking-frames and bricks—and Dissent—began to make something new out of the old and ragged town of Leicester.

FURTHER INFORMATION

The available information for this period is almost all included in James Thompson's *History of Leicester*, and in *Records of the Borough of Leicester* (edited by E. M. Bateson up to 1603 and by Helen Stocks from 1603 to 1688).

C. J. Billson's *Mediæval Leicester*, however, extends into the period which has here been called Tudor.

Leicester during the Great Civil War, by J. F. Hollings (1840), gives a detailed and clear account of the military operations in the siege which has not, as far as I know, been superseded. This account was used in Mrs. Fielding Johnson's *Glimpses of Ancient Leicester* which is easier to obtain. A more recent publication on this topic is *The Siege of Leicester: 1645*, by S. Green and J. Wilshere (1972).

William Kelly's writings, notably his *Royal Progresses* and his *Notices Illustrative of the Drama*, are interesting and informative though his grounds for accepting current traditions are not always substantial.

The death of Wolsey is fully described in *The Life of Cardinal Wolsey* attributed to George Cavendish, his gentleman usher. (The original manuscript, edited by S. W. Singer, F.S.A., Second Edition, London, Harding, Triphook and Lepard, 1825; also Folio Society, 1962).

For the Stewardship of the Honor of Leicester, see articles by Mr. (later Dr.) Levi Fox in *Transactions of the Leicestershire Archaeological Society*, Vols. XIX, XX, and XXI.

TUDOR AND STUART PERIODS
DATES FOR REFERENCE

General History		*Leicester*	
A.D.		A.D.	
1485	Accession of Henry VII		Burial of Richard III
		1489	Election of burgesses to Parliament ordered to be by 'the forty-eight only and not by the Commonalty'
		1494	Corporation meets in Corpus Christi Hall
1509	Accession of Henry VIII		
		1513	Foundation of Wyggeston's Hospital
1514	Wolsey Archbishop of York and chief Minister of State		
		1530	Death of Wolsey at Leicester Abbey
1533	Denial of papal supremacy and divorce of Katherine of Aragon		

77

General History		Leicester	
A.D.		A.D.	
1537	Dissolution of smaller monasteries		
		1538–9	Dissolution and destruction of Leicester Abbey
		1545–6	Guilds and Chantries dissolved
1547	Accession of Edward VI		Church ornaments and vestments sold
1553	Accession of Queen Mary		
		1556	Thomas Moore burned as a heretic
1558	Accession of Queen Elizabeth		
		1573	Foundation of Free Grammar School
1577–80	Drake sails round the world		
1588	The Spanish Armada	1588	Charter of Incorporation
		1593	Visitation of Plague
1603	Accession of James I		
		1610–11	Plague prevalent
1625	Accession of Charles I	1625–6	Plague prevalent
		1628	Enclosure of Leicester Forest
		1632	Town Library founded
1642	Civil War begins		
1645	Battle of Naseby	1645	Siege and Capture of Leicester by Royalists: resurrender to Parliamentarians in same year
1649	Execution of Charles I		
1660	Restoration of Charles II		
		1661	Freemen claim right to vote in Parliamentary elections
1662	Act of Uniformity		
1665	Plague in London		
1666	Fire of London		
1667	Dutch fleet in Medway		
		1680?	First Stocking-frame in Leicester
1685	Accession of James II		
1688	Abdication of James II		
1689	Accession of William and Mary		

Section II

TUDOR AND STUART BUILDINGS

NEITHER the Tudor nor the Stuart period was an age which, in Leicester, produced many new buildings, nor were the buildings which it did produce of a kind which were likely to survive. The general level of domestic convenience must have improved greatly, but as long as the main frames of the houses were wooden most of the work would consist of adding chimney breasts, partitioning internally and inserting or adding upper storeys. The few mansions which were built—notably the one in the Grey Friars, the 'Lord's Place' of the Earls of Huntingdon in the (present) High Street and the Cavendish House on the Abbey Site—have all gone, except for some ruined walls of the last named.

Just a few important buildings remain, however, which typify public and upper-class domestic life during these periods.

It might perhaps be more correct to describe the timbered hall of what was 18 Highcross Street as late medieval than as Tudor. It may have been built for Roger Wygston the Younger (died 1542) but it was the kind of house in which a wealthy Tudor or Stuart merchant was glad and even proud to live in. I have therefore preferred to notice it in this section though it may be contemporary with William Wyggeston's Chantry House in the Newarke which was not built till 1512 but which was specifically related to the medieval foundation of the collegiate church.

In the early nineteen-seventies, Roger Wygston's House was restored by the Museums Service after having been in a poor state of repair for a number of years. The timbered wall looks out over a courtyard, the entrance being by the side of the eighteenth century façade which faces the street. The street is no longer known as Highcross Street, but the busy St. Nicholas Circle. The volume of traffic passing the door has had to be taken into account in the restoration of the building, both in the preservation of the fabric itself and in the protection of the attractive displays of costume through the ages for which the building now provides ideal room settings. Also on show are shop scenes; a shoe shop, a draper's and a milliner's, of the nineteen-twenties. The fine stained glass windows of the house have not been put back in place during the restoration, due to the difficulty of ensuring their safety, but they are preserved in the Jewry Wall and Newarke Houses Museums.

Roger Wygston's House is open to the public on weekdays 10 a.m. to 5.30 p.m. and on Sundays 2 p.m. to 5.30 p.m.

The Old Town Hall (now known as the Guildhall) and the adjoining Library were also, in part, built before this period and altered and added to after it.

The whole complex of buildings on this site is concisely described in Fosbrooke and Skillington's History as follows:

> The hall and its appurtenant structures comprise a set of miscellaneous buildings which enclose an uncovered rectangular court. The largest of these, the great hall, stands on the north side of the quadrangle, and is separated by its outer wall from the narrow thoroughfare called Town Hall Lane. The three eastern bays of the room were built about 1400, and formed the original hall of the Corpus Christi brotherhood. About 1450, the gild

having increased its membership and improved its financial position, the original hall was extended westwards by the addition of two more bays. Some fifty years later, a second hall was built, on the west side of the courtyard, at right-angles to the western portion of the great hall, i.e., to the two bays added in the middle of the fifteenth century. This second hall was erected about the time when the principal meetings of the borough council began to be held in the great hall of the gild, and it is not unlikely that its cost was defrayed by the ruling burgesses. The kitchens, etc., stood on the south side of the yard, opposite to the main hall, and the houses of the four priests who served at the gild's altar in St. Martin's are said to have occupied the east side, and so to have completed the square; but of this there is no proof. Soon after 1563, when the gild premises became the property of the town, the western hall was converted into a three-storey building, with two gables facing the courtyard. The room on the ground floor became the mayor's parlour, and the attic over the first floor was formed by the insertion of a floor at the tie-beam level of the roof. In 1637, the mayor's parlour and the room above it—the one now occupied by the Leicestershire Archaeological Society—were 'new built', and the mayor's seat and the elaborately carved chimney-piece in the parlour were fixed in their places at the same time. The buildings in which the town library is stored were erected about 1632, and were afterwards 'beautified' and extended by Alderman Newton and others. The brick house on the south side of the court, formerly occupied by the chief constable, dates from about 1840, as do the cells and other police buildings which appear on the plans.

The Guildhall is open to the public on weekdays 10 a.m. to 5.30 p.m. and on Sundays 2 p.m. to 5.30 p.m.

Close to the before-mentioned buildings, in Highcross Street but on the far side of High Street is the old Free Grammar School, built in 1573 out of the ruins of St. Peter's Church. It is now used for bus company offices. Both ends have been shorn off and replaced with modern walls, and the rest of the building, considerably restored, has no pretensions to architectural grandeur. It is, however, an interesting piece of building in Forest stone and Swithland slate, constituting a relief to the eye amongst acres of dull brickwork which at least one person who passes it daily would be very sorry to lose.

As a happy conclusion to a short list, there are the Newarke Houses adjoining Wyggeston's Chantry House. These are probably, in the main, Jacobean and their rooms, one of which is panelled, form a gracious setting for furniture and pictures of that date as well as for a collection of agricultural and household 'bygones' and other objects appropriate to their use as a museum of Leicestershire social history.

The Newarke Houses are open to the public at the same hours as the Guildhall.

Wherever they lived, Tudor and Stuart citizens came at last to the churchyard or the family vault and there the local mason inscribed above them their names and what was noteworthy in their lives.

Every old church has some of these memorials and in St. Martin's a whole congregation of departed worthies, led by the Herricks, make a brave stand against oblivion.

FURTHER INFORMATION

THE GUILDHALL. C. J. Billson's *Mediæval Leicester*, Chapter V, gives an account of the history of the use of the hall and in the appendix (pp. 216-17) cites a full list of authorities, in particular an article in the *Journal of the British Archaeological Association*, 1863, by Gordon Hills, and one by William Kelly on 'The Old Guildhalls of Leicester' in *Spencer's Almanack*, 1879.

The most recent, most complete and fully authoritative account is, however, *The Old Town Hall, Leicester*, by T. H. Fosbrooke, F.S.A., and S. H. Skillington (1925). This includes architectural plans prepared by Messrs. Fosbrooke and Bedingfield during the work of restoration and preservation.

The books in the old Library are catalogued and described in *The Old Town Hall Library of Leicester*, by Cecil Deedes, M.A., J. E. Stocks, D.D., and J. L. Stocks, M.A. (Oxford, printed for the Corporation of Leicester, 1919). This also gives a brief account of the buildings. The history of the library is given in Phillip G. Lindley's *The Town Library of Leicester* (Upton, Wirral, 1975).

WYGSTON'S HOUSE (18 Highcross Street) is noticed in Billson's *Mediæval Leicester*, which cites an account by Thomas North of the glass in L.A.S., IV, 138. Illustration, p. 149, description, p. 208). There is a notice and illustration also in Mrs. Fielding Johnson's *Glimpses of Ancient Leicester*, p. 119 (second edition). A full and authoritative account of the glass by G. McN. Rushforth was published in *The Archaeological Journal*, Vol. LXXV (Second Series, Vol. XXV), pp. 47-68, 1918. Also on this topic is *Painted Glass from Leicester* (Museums, 1962). Plans and elevations of the house were published in *The Forty-fourth Annual Report of the Leicester Society of Architects* (1917) where the house is dated 1500-50.

NEWARKE HOUSES (and Chantry). These are noticed in Billson's *Mediæval Leicester*, p. 206-7, and in *The Newarke, its Origin and Associations*, by S. H. Skillington (1912). This pamphlet was written to support the appeal then being launched for the purchase and preservation of the houses.

Section III

(a) JOHN LELAND[1]

[JOHN Leland was almost the first serious and systematic observer of the antiquities of England. His 'Laborious journey' comprised a number of journeys up and down the country and is an invaluable record of what was to be seen just after the Middle Ages had ended. It is interesting to note that he apparently did not inspect, and hardly mentions, the Abbey,

[1] The Itinerary of John Leland
the Antiquary.
Vol the First
Publish'd from the Original MS in the Bodleian Library
by Thomas Hearne, M.A.
3rd In.
Oxford MDCC LXVIII.
P16 seq. Fol. 16 seq.

which was on the point of being dissolved. Perhaps visitors, just then, were not welcomed.]

The Hole Toune of *Leircester* at this Tyme is buildid of tymbre: and so is *Lughborow* after the same rate.

S. John's Hospital Landes for the most part was given by *Edward* the 4. to the College of *Newark* in *Leyrcester*.

Other *Robert Bossue,* Erle of Leircester, or *Petronilla,* a Countess of *Leircester,* was buried in a Tumbe *ex marmore calchedonica* yn the Waul of the South of the High Altar of *S. Mairie* Abbay of *Leyrcester*.

The Waulles of *S. Marie* Abbay be 3 quarters of Mile aboute.

The *Gray-Freres* of *Leircester* stode at the ende of the Hospital of Mr. *Wigeston. Simon de Mountefort,* as I lernid, was Founder there: and there was byried King *Richard* 3 and a Knight caulled Mutton, sumtyme Mayre of Leycester.

I saw in the Quire of the *Blake-Freres* the Tumbe of ....And a flat Alabaster Stone with the name of Lady *Isabel* Wife to *Sr John Beauchamp* of HO(lt). And in the North Isle I saw the Tumbe of another Knight without Scripture. And in the North Crosse Isle (a Tombe) having the Name of Roger Po(ynter) of *Leircester* armid . . .

These things brevely I markid at
           Leyrcester.

The Castelle stonding nere the West Bridge is at this Tyme a thing of small Estimation: and there is no Apparaunce other of high Waulles or Dikes. So that I think that the Lodginges that now be there were made sins the Tyme of the Barons War in Henry the 3. Tyme; and great likelihod there is That the Castelle was much defacid in Henry the 2. Tyme when the Waulles of *Leircester* were defacid.

There was afor the Conqueste a Collegiate Chirch of Prebendes *intra Castrum.* The Landes where of gyven by *Robert Bossu* Erle of *Leircestre* to the Abbay of Chanons made by him withoute the Waulles. a new Chirch of the Residew of the old Prebendes was erectid withoute the Castelle, and dedicate to *S. Marie* as the olde was.

In this Chirch of S. *Marie extra castrum* I saw the Tumbe of Marble of *Thomas Rider,* Father of Master *Richard of Leicester.* This Richard I take to be the same that yn those Dayes, as it apperith by his Workes, was a great Clerke. Beside this Grave I saw few thinges there of any auncient Memorie within the Chirch.

The Collegiate Chirch of *Newarke* and the Area of it yoinith to a nother Peace of the Castelle Ground.

The College Chirch is not very great, but it is exceeding fair.

There lyith on the North side of the High Altare *Henry* Erle of *Lancaster,* withowt a Crounet, and 2 Men children under the Arche next to his Hedde.

On the Southe side lyith *Henry* the first Duke of *Lancaster*: and yn the next Arch to his Hedde lyith a Lady, by likelihod hif Wife.

Constance, Doughtter to *Peter*, King of *Castelle*, and Wife to *John of Gaunt*, liith after the High Altare in a Tumbe of Marble with an Image of (Brasse) (like a Quene) on it.

There is a Tumbe of Marble in the Body of the Quire. They told me that a Countess of *Darby* lay biried on it, and they make her, I wot not how, Wife to *John of Gaunt or* Henry the 4. Indeade Henry the 4 wille *John of Gaunt* lived was callid Erle of *Darby*.

In the Chapelle of St. *Mary* on the Southe side of the Quire ly buried to of the Shirleys, Knights with their Wives; and one Brokesby an *Esquier*. Under a Piller yn a Chapelle of the South Crosse Isle lyith the Lady *Hungreford*, and *Sacheverel* her Secund Husbande.

In the Southside of the Body of the Chirch lyith one of the *Bluntes*, a Knight, with his Wife.

And on the North side of the Chirch ly 3 Wigstons, greate Benefactors to the College. one of them was a Prebendarie there, and made the free Grammar Schole.

The Cloistor on the South Weste side of the Chirch is large and faire: and the Houses in the Cumpace of the Area of the College for the Prebendaries be al very praty.

The Waulles and Gates of the College be stately.

The riche Cardinal of *Winchester* gildid al the Floures and Knottes in the Voulte of the Chirch.

The large Almose House stondith also withyn the Quadrante of the Area of the College.

A little above the West bridge the *Sore* castith oute an Arme, and sone after it cummith in again, and makith one streame of *Sore*.

Withyn this Isle standith the Blake-Freres very pleasauntly, and hard by the Freres is also a Bridge of Stone over this Arme of Sore. And after the hole Water creping aboute half the Toune cummith thorough the North Bridge of a VIj or VIIj Arches of (Stone). And there *Sore* brek(eth into two) armes againe, wher(of the biggest) goith by *S. Maries* a(bbay standing) on the farther Ripe; and the other, caullid *the Bishoppes Water*, bycause the Bishop of Lincoln's Tenantes have Privilege on it, and after sone melthith with the bigger Arme, and so insulatith a right large and plesaunt Meadow; wherapon the Abbay, as I suppose, in sum Writings is caullid *S. Maria de pratis*. Over the Middle Part of this Arme of *Bishops Water* is a meane Stone bridge: and a little beyond it is a nother Stone bridge, thorough the which passit a little land broke, cumming from Villages not far of, and so rennith into *Bishops Water*. And by Bishops Water is a Chapel longging to the Hospital of S. *John*. At this Chapel lyith *Mr. Boucher*.

S. Margarete's is thereby the fairest Paroche Chirch of Leircester, wher ons was Cathedrale Chirch and thereby the Bishop of *Lincoln* had a Palace, whereof a little yet standeth.

John Peny first Abbate of Leircester, then Bishop of *Bangor* and *Cairluel* (is here buried in) an Alabaster Tumbe. (This *Penny* made the new Bricke workes of Leicester Abby, and much of the brick waulles.)

From *Leircester to Bradgate* by ground welle wooddid 3 Miles. At *Bradgate* is a fair Parke and a Lodge lately buildid there by the Lorde *Thomas Grey,* Marquis of *Dorsete,* Father to *Henry* that is now Marquise . . . . . .

FORESTES YN LEIRCESTERSHIRE

The foreste of *Leyrcester* yoining hard to the Toune: it is a V Miles lenghthe, but no greate Breede: and is replensihed with Dere.

The Foreste of *Charley* a XX Miles in Cumpace.

PARKES YN LEYRCESTERSHIRE

The Parke by *S. Mary* Abbay. The *Frith* Park sumtyme a light large thyng, now partly deparkid, and partely bering the Name of the *New Park,* welle palid.

Bellemontes Lease sumtyne a great Park by Leircester but now convertid to Pasture.

Barne Parke, and *Towley* Park, and Beewmanor. Al these be the Kinges.   etc.

(b) RICHARD SYMONDS[1]

(1645)

[Symonds came of a gentleman's family of Gt. Yeldham, Essex, and was in a troop of horse under Lord Bernard Stuart, son of the Duke of Lennox.]

[1645] Thursday [May 29] his Majestie [coming from Cotes nr Loughborough] marched and pitcht down before Leicester citty, a garrison of the rebells, and commanded by Theoph. Grey, third brother to the Earle of Kent.

Friday May 30. His Highness Prince Rupert sent a trumpet (after he had shott two great pieces at the towne) to summon it for his Majestie,

[1]Diary
of the
Marches of the Royal Army during the great Civil War
kept by
Richard Symonds
Now first published from the original MS. in the British Museum
ed. by
Charles Edward Long, M.A.
Printed for the Camden Society
MDCCCLIX

offering the burgesses and corporacion pardon, &c. They deteyne his trumpet, and about one of the clock afternoone, in this interim, the Prince rayses a battery for six great pieces upon a hill, where sometymes of old had byn such another. About two of the clock, one of the Leicester trumpets was sent to desire time to consider of it till the morrow morning and to tell him that they wondered he would rayse any worke &c during this summons. His Highness told the trumpet if he came agen with such another errand he'd lay him by the heels. About half an houre after he comes agen with this note directed thus: 'To the Commander in Cheife' desiring time to consider till the morrow morning.

The Prince commits the trumpet to his Marshall. Still the first trumpet they keepe. Then the Prince about three of the clock sent them an answer in lowder termes; six great peices from the fort on the south side of the towne playing on a stone wall unlyned, and made ere six of the clock a breach of great space. Musketts and cannon continually putting us in mind of some thing done.

The towne of Leicester was cheifely governed by a committee, vizt. Mr. Huett of Dunton; Mr. Haslerigg; Ludlom, a chandler there; Mr. Payne of Medbourne; Newton of Houghton, a receiver, some time high constable; Read of Thirlby; Mr. Lewyn; . . . Stanley, a mercer there by the West Gate:

Sir Robert Pye of Farringdon came two or three dayes [before] into the towne, and was a great means of resisting the Prince.

After the breach was made in the wall by our cannon, by six of the clock, they in the towne had gotten up a handsome retrenchment with three flankers (a great Spanish peice) within four or five yards of the wall.

All the evening was a general preparation to assaulte the towne, and a little before 12 of the clock in the night this violent storm began, and continued till after one. Colonel George Lisle's tertia fell on upon the breach; once beate off, and the King sent his foot regiment of lifeguards, to assist, but they gott fully in before.

Colonel Bard's tertia fell on with scaling ladders, some neare a flanker, and others scaled the horne worke before the drawbridge on the east side.

Sir Bernard Asteleyes tertia fell on, on the north side, which is the river side, and a draw [bridge] next the abbey.

Colonel John Russell, with the Prince's regiment of blew cotes, and also the Prince's fferelockes, assaulted.

They sett the Prince's black colours on the great battery within. Earl of Northampton's horse about one of the clock were lett in at the ports and they scowred the lyne and towne. In the meane time the foot gott in and fell to plunder, so that ere day fully open scarse a cottage unplundered. There were many Scotts in this toune, and no quarter was given to any in the heat.

More dead bodyes lay just within the lyne farre then without or in the graffe.

I told 30 and more at the breach, as many within as without. Every street had some. I believe 200 on both sides were not killed.

Wee lost Colonel St. George. Major Bunnington, gentleman pensioner, shott in the eye just as he was on the top of the ladder. 28 or 30 officers. Major of the Prince Rupert's firelocks.

The army of horse faced in bodyes all night in severall places. About day 10 of the enemy gott out and escaped by the river side; were followed.

[Here follows the order of the Army of Horse, then a note of the principal houses in Leicestershire] His Majestie quartered this Friday night at Leicester Abbey, the Countess of Devon's howse. [Here follows a note of the antiquities and monuments of Ashby-de-la-Zouch Church.]

His Majestie rested at Leicester Abbey, the army of foot in Leicester, the horse round about in dorpes and villages.

[The King then marched to relieve Oxford.]

The county of Leicester is generally champaigne pasture and erable, little or no wast, and small wood; some quick hedges, and the parishes stand less than one myle distant.

[After Naseby 14 June, 1645.]

The horse escaped to Leicester this afternoone and were pursued by a body of the enemyes horse and loose scowters to Great Glyn, and there the Earle of Lichfield charged their loose men with halfe a score horse and beate them back.

[Then comes a list of killed.]

Towards night this dismall Satterday, his Majestie, after the wounded were taken care for in Leicester, and that the two Princes were come safe to him, and had taken order with that garrison, and left two regiments of horse there, viz. the Queenes and Colonel Caryes, he marched that night (for now wee had left running), to Ashby-de-la-Zouch.

. . . . . .

The day before we came to Hereford [i.e. on 17 June] His Majestie had intelligence that Fairfax had appeared before Leicester, and that Lord Loughborough had yielded it upon conditions.

To march away the soldjers, sans armes, officers with swords.

Two regiments of horse, vizt. Queenes and Caryes; the men marched, but horses and armes the enemy had.

1,500 foot marched out of Leicester withe those gentlemen and wounded men that came in I suppose.

(c) JOHN EVELYN[1]
(1654)

[John Evelyn, b. 1620, d. 1706, is well known from his *Diary* and other works. He was a learned and cultivated man and held a number of public offices under the later Stuarts. His visit to Leicester was made during a tour of several months during which he visited various relatives; he was not primarily sightseeing.]

Aug. 4. Hence riding thro' a considerable part of Leicestershire, an open, rich, but unpleasant country, we came late in the evening to Horninghold, a seate of my wife's unkle.

Aug. 7. Went to Uppingham, the Shire-towne of Rutland, pretty & well-builte of stone, which is a rarity in that part of England, where most of the rural parishes are but of mud, and the people living as wretchedly as in the most impoverished parts of France, which they much resemble, being idle and sluttish. The country (especially Leicestershire) much in common; the gentry free drinkers.

Aug. 9. To the old & ragged Citty of Leicester, large & pleasantly seated, but despicably built, the chimney flues like so many smiths' forges; however famous for the tombe of the Tyrant Richard the Third, which is now converted to a cistern, at which (I think) cattel drink. Also here in one of the Churches lies buried the magnificent Cardinal Wolsey.

John of Gaunt has here also built a large, but poore Hospital, neere which a wretch has made him an house out of the ruins of a stately church. Saw the ruins of an old Roman Temple, thought to be of Janus. Entertain'd at a very fine collation of fruits, such as I did not expect to meet with so far North, especially very good melons. We returned to my unkle's.

(d) CELIA FIENNES[2]
(c. 1700)

['Celia Fiennes was the daughter of Colonel Nathaniel Fiennes, a Parliamentarian Officer, by his marriage with Miss Whitehead, and was sister of the third Viscount Saye and Sele'.

[1] Diary of John Evelyn Esq., F.R.S.
Edited from the Original MSS. by William Bray, F.S.A.,
New edition by Henry B. Wheatley, F.S.A.,
London, Bickers & Son, 1906.

[2] Through England on a Side Saddle
in the time of William & Mary
being the diary of
Celia Fiennes
With an introduction by
The Hon. Mrs. Griffiths
LONDON: Field & Tuer, the Leadenhall Press, E.C.
Simpkin, Marshall & Co: Hamilton Adams & Co.
NEW YORK: Scribner & Welford, 743 & 745, Broadway.

The date of this visit to Leicester is not mentioned, but in the book, which is a copy of the original MS., *My Great Journey to Newcastle and to Cornwall,* in the course of which it occurred, follows an account of two other tours which occupied the year 1697. The book itself was put together not long after the coronation of Queen Anne—of which she was a spectator and gives a detailed account.]

Thence [from Wansford] I went to Durant(1) 5 miles and passed over a very good stone bridge. Here we are near ye quarry's of stone and all ye houses and walls are built of stone as in Gloucestershire.

This River and bridge Enter'd me into Leicestershire wch is a very Rich Country—Red land, good Corne of all sorts and grass, both fields and jnclosures. You see great way upon their hills ye bottoms full of Enclosures, woods and different sort of manureing and Herbage, amongst wch are placed many little towns wch gives great pleasure of ye travellers to view. Y^e miles are long but hither its pretty hard good way; to Coppingham(2) 5 miles more wch is a neate market town. Satturday is their market wch is very good affording great quantetyes of Corn, leather garne(3) and Cattle; such a Concourse of people y^t my Landlord told me he used to have 100 horse set up at his jnn, and there were many publick houses. Here you see very large fine sheep and very good land, but very deep bad roads.

From hence to Leister wch they Call but 13 miles, but ye longest 13 I ever went and ye most tiresome being full of sloughs, y^t I was near 11 hours going but 25 miles, as they Reckon it, between Wansford and Leicester(4) town—a footman Could have gone much faster than I Could Ride. Their fewell here is as I said but Cowdung or Coale wch they are supplyed with out of Warwickshire, Leicester town stands on the Side of a little riseing Ground, tho' at a distance from ye adjacent hills it Looks Low, but its a good prospect. It has 4 gates, ye streetes are pretty Large and well pitch'd, there are five parishes; the Market place is a Large space very handsome wth a good Market Cross and town hall. Y^e river Sow wch runs into ye river Reeke and both Empts themselves into ye Trent. Trent to ye Bow Bridge which is one arch over into ye Priory, wch King Rich^d ye third pass'd over out of ye Priory when he went to fight in Bowsorth field wth King Henry the seventh, but the stone he struck his heele at and against wch his head was struck at his return when brought athwart the horse Dead, I Could not se it, being removed, but I saw a piece of his tombstone he lay in, wch was Cut out in exact form for his body to Lye in; y^t remains to be seen at ye Greyhound in Leicester but is partly broken(5). There I saw a piece of ye jury wall as its Called being in arches and was a place where the Jews burnt their sacrifices.

There are two Hospitalls, one for old men ye other women 24 in number; they are allowed 2s. 8d. pr week, Candle, fewell oatmeale, butter and salt. I saw the Library wch is pretty large, there are two Large

Divinity Books the arch-Bishop gave them lately, and the names of all their Benefactors; there was one book all written hand by a scribe before printing was found out, it was a fine vellum; and there was another Book of ye New Testament in Chineaze Language & Characteur.(6) Y^e town is old timber building Except one or two of Brick. There is Indeed that they call ye Newark wch is Encompass'd wth a wall of a good thickness and two great gates wth towers as the town gates are, in wch they keep their arms and amunition. Y^e walls now are only to secure gardens that are made of ye ruin'd places that were buildings of strength. In this Newark wch is a large space of ground are severall good houses some of stone and Brick In which some Lawyers live ffrank;(7) there is also a new pile of Building all of Brick wch is the Guild Hall where ye assizes are kept twice in ye yeare and ye session quarterly.(8)

St Martins Church wch is one of ye biggest—there is none very big and none fine—but here I saw Hyricks tomb who was major of ye town and was married to one wife 52 years in all, wch tyme he buried neither man woman or Child tho' most tymes he had 20 on his family, his age was 79 and his widow 97 at her death, she saw 142 of her posterity together. They have a water-house and a water mill to turn ye water in deep Leaden tubbs or Cisterns for their use: there are wells in some streetes to draw water by a hand wheele for ye Common use of the town.

The major and alderman goes about in procession on Holy Thursday which was ye day I was there.(9) Here are a great many descenters in this town. This Country as I s^d was all Rich deep land, and they plough their land all wth ploughs w^thout wheeles as they do in Oxfordshire and other deep lands.

NOTES

(1) Presumably Duddington.

(2) Presumably Uppingham.

(3) 'garne' is probably a dialect version of 'yarn' though this variant is only recorded from northern counties.

(4) As *we* reckon it, the distance from Wansford to Leicester is 33 miles and from Uppingham to Leicester 19 miles.

(5) According to other reporters, however, the stone reputed to have been Richard III's coffin or tombstone stood in front of the White Horse Inn in Gallowtree gate. It is said to have been broken up in the time of George I.

(6) The hand-written book was probably the library's 13th Century MS. of the Vulgate: the other may have been the Codex Leicestrensis (a Greek New Testament in uncial characters). There is no record of any book in Chinese: Throsby speaks of a New Testament translated into the Indian Language, Cambridge 1671, and of a Hebrew book in Syriac characters believed by the common people to have been written by Christ or one of the Apostles which was shown to every visitor as a curious relic. There is an old Hebrew Bible in the Library now.

(7) I discovered by chance (from a quotation in Mr. S. H. Skillington's *The Newarke & its Associations*) that the Rev. Samuel Carte, writing about 1712, notes of the Newarke: 'There are three very fair houses belonging to *William Franke Esq.*, Lawrence Carter Esq., and Mrs. Stephens.'

(8) This must, I think, refer to the new brick front of the Castle where the County Sessions were held.

(9) The very Catholic procession on Corpus Christi Day (the first Thursday after Trinity) seems, from this, to have lasted on as a civic ceremony in spite of the Reformation and the puritanism of the Commonwealth.

PART IV

EIGHTEENTH AND NINETEENTH CENTURY LEICESTER

EIGHTEENTH AND NINETEENTH CENTURY LEICESTER

THE history of a town is the history of its differences from other towns. The justification, if there is one, for including eighteenth and nineteenth century Leicester in a single essay is the fact that as early as 1700 it was becoming clear that the town's future would be that of a manufacturing centre. The justification, if there is one, for including both centuries in an account of ancient Leicester is the fact that even in 1900 there were in Leicester many ways of life, some streets and a few buildings that had nothing to do with manufacturing and that would never have been there at all if Leicester had been a wholly new town, begotten by private enterprise out of the industrial revolution. Because Leicester was still a county town and an important market for corn, cattle, and other local country produce, there was always a nucleus of people who were independent of the town's main industries, and, in consequence, its planned or unplanned development has been a little less one-sided than would otherwise have been the case.

Many other old towns were changing, at the beginning of the eighteenth century, into centres of manufacture, but Leicester's manner of doing so was unusual if not unique. In most cases there was some obvious natural advantage that could be turned to account; coal or iron or, in the case of the textile industries, water power. Leicester had none of these and the stocking-frame on which her industry was built was not a 'machine' in the sense that this was ordinarily understood, as something that was operated by harnessing some natural source of power, but a mechanical device which, like a bicycle, extended and multiplied human effort. So little help did Leicester obtain from the accident of her situation that one is almost tempted to seek in the forceful character of their Danish ancestry an explanation of the fact that her citizens started in the race for production and population so very much sooner than other old Midlands towns like Coventry and Oxford.

Whether it was a good thing to start so early, or to start at all, must be a matter of opinion. No doubt it would have been pleasanter for a few people if Leicester had grown no more than Warwick, whilst a late development of industrialism might have been accompanied by greater efforts to preserve some of the best features of the old town. But the thought of the amorphous growth that might, in the first case, have enveloped some Leicestershire village and the utter disunity of plan and purpose that would perplex us in the second, may make us, on the whole, moderately grateful that events took the course they did.

A direct consequence of the fact that Leicester's first industry was established without power-driven machinery was that for a very long time production was not crowded into factories and has never been concentrated into very large factories. The one thing in which the hosiery industry came into line with others was the adoption of the capitalist technique: men worked at frames and with material that belonged to their employers. They continued, in the old way, to work in their own homes and it was not necessary that their homes should be close together or even that they should be in the town itself. This again was a mixed blessing if it was a blessing at all. Leicester was saved from festering slums but not from spreading acres of mean cottages, and Leicestershire villages became prosperous but ceased to be either rural or beautiful. Home conditions of labour were sometimes better, but sometimes worse than factory conditions. The workers maintained some independence of outlook but paid heavily for it in a greater insecurity of employment and the necessity of accepting conditions from the capitalist which were often iniquitous. The worst feature of the trade was the fact that workmen were obliged to pay rent for the frames at a fixed rate, whatever the price they got for their work and even when the masters did not give out enough yarn to keep them fully occupied.

Probably as far as the workers themselves were concerned, the development of the knitting industry brought more benefit to those in the ancillary occupations of spinning and woolcombing than to the knitters themselves. Spinning was largely a country task, providing a modest supplement to the income of farmers' and farm labourers' households. Woolcombing seems to have been recognized as a quite important feature of working life in Leicester. A grand procession organized in 1763 to celebrate the conclusion of peace with France included (after a number of Masonic representatives):

The Bishop,
In an open landau, drawn by six horses, with three postillions and
four pages, all habited. His lordship in a
gown and cassock, a mitre of wool on his
head; in one hand the Book of Common
Prayer, in the other a woolcomb.[1]
A Shepherd and Shepherdess on horseback.
Another Shepherd and Shepherdess.
A stage, built on a waggon, with two combers at work, two doublers,
two spinners, a framework-knitter at his calling, and a crown
of wool on the stage.
A procession of about twenty combers, all habited in wool wigs,
sashes, ruffled shirts, and grey stockings, three and three.

[1] The association of 'the Bishop' with woolcombers may have been a reminiscence of medieval traditions of pageantry. Bishop Blaize was their patron saint. (He was Blasius, an Armenian bishop, who was martyred A.D. 316 by having his flesh scored with iron combs before he was beheaded.)

It is evident that, by this time, Leicester felt that it had made a substantial, even a notable industry out of what were, after all, the leavings of the woollen trade. The lack of outstanding natural advantages had not prevented the rapidly increasing local population from finding suitable industrial employment but it had, very fortunately, prevented the growth of industry from being so rapid as to require wholesale immigration of labour to keep pace with an insatiable demand for its products. For very many sad years, gangs of pauper children from London and elsewhere were sent by the overseers for 'apprenticeship' in the northern woollen mills. There may have been abuses of the pauper apprenticeship system in Leicester—it is said that in a particular class of small worsted hose the work was done chiefly by paupers and that it was 'very bad for the nerves'—but things were not likely to go quite so frightfully wrong when overseers and masters lived in the same town as when they were hundreds of miles apart. Whilst the weight of English wealth and population was shifting from south to north, far too rapidly to allow an orderly adjustment of living conditions, a Midlands town had as good a chance as any to grow without degenerating into a slum. Immigration to Leicester there certainly was, and at some periods a great deal, but it was chiefly from those Leicestershire villages which for one reason or another (but generally from the controlling landowner's refusal to allow it) did not themselves grow into miniature hosiery-manufacturing towns.

There is no doubt that the old aim, often expressed by Tudor and Stuart corporations, of finding a means 'to set the poor on work' had an important influence in bringing the hosiery trade to Leicester. To this extent there was planned development but accident and individual initiative took the development far beyond the plan and left the Corporation as helpless and ridiculous as a hen that has hatched a gosling. The Town Council made some effort to restrict the trade to freemen and their apprentices but it was overruled and by the end of the century it had lost its power to restrict or to do much to regulate any trade at all.

As it became less and less responsible for the conduct of trade affairs, the Corporation became more and more corrupt and inefficient, more and more inclined to care only for the personal interests of its own exclusive membership. This is the aspect that has been stressed by the historians who represented the victorious party. It was not so clear to contemporaries that the advocates of the new order had all the right on their side. A serious and responsible body of opinion, perhaps even for a time the majority in Leicester, agreed with the Corporation that the 'Glorious Revolution' of 1688 had been a disastrous and shameful blunder. When in the '45 Rebellion the Pretender reached Derby there were many good men ready and willing to give him a loyal welcome at his next stopping place on the way to London; there would have been more if his following had included a larger proportion of gentry and yeomen from the northern counties of England and fewer wild and predatory Highlanders.[1] Only just saved by the turn of events from laying themselves open to a charge of treason, the Corporation and its supporters were left in a hopelessly weak position. They no longer dared to assert their authority to resist the claim of the new men to manage their new trade in the way that seemed best to themselves. And as time went on these new men became the majority, if you exclude, as both sides excluded, the manual workers from serious consideration. They comprised not only the hosiers and frame-owners but an increasing number of merchants, shopkeepers, and craftsmen who lived by the new industry, and, perhaps most important of all, the bankers who stood behind every venture.[2]

All that was left for the Corporation to do was to look after its own property, or what it held to be its own property, and to maintain and improve the public services. The latter function it performed not badly, considering that with very limited funds it had to look after a great many new needs which the people who were responsible for creating them thought (if we may judge by their behaviour in wholly new industrial areas) they were under no obligation to provide for. Leicester entered the nineteenth century with at least the basic advantage of paved and lighted streets, properly regulated markets, covered public pumps and a small supply of piped water, available at 'the Conduit' near what is now Victoria Parade. Very early in the century the Corporation had undertaken a rehousing scheme, ordering a number of houses belonging to the town to be pulled down and 'convenient small tenements' to be erected in their place, and it would be possible to make quite an imposing list of the public buildings that were put up. Almost all their work was superseded, demolished, and forgotten when the next century made much broader schemes imperative, but one piece of their planning, the New Walk, or as some then called it, Queen's Walk, still earns the gratitude of pedestrians.

Leicester's inheritance of private benefactions, as well as those of new men who, in this respect, followed the good old tradition, did much to make up for municipal deficiencies. Wyggeston's Hospital, the Trinity and St. John's Hospitals (the latter supplemented by Bent's Charity) and Sir Thomas White's loans as well as many minor bequests continued, in spite of some instances of maladministration, to relieve the old and assist the young. About 1760 Alderman Gabriel Newton, a crusty but benevolent eccentric, endowed a school where boys were not only able to

---

[1] Some of them came nearer than Derby: Sir Robert Martin has preserved a charming story of a very old man in Anstey who, as a boy, had been captured and ill-treated by a foraging party. In his dotage he was inclined to wander off, and children sent to fetch him used to make a noise like the bagpipes. As soon as he heard it he always made for home as fast as his legs would carry him!

[2] There is a full account of the old Leicester banks in C. J. Billson's *Leicester Memoirs*.

OLD WEST BRIDGE, FROM FLOWERS' LITHOGRAPH OF ABOUT 1830

HIGHCROSS STREET ABOUT 1830, FROM THE FLOWERS' LITHOGRAPH. OF THE BUILDINGS SHOWN ABOVE, THERE REMAIN ONLY THE SHOP DATED 1717, A FRAGMENT OF THE WALL OF THE OLD GAOL BEYOND IT, AND THE OLD FREE SCHOOL, NOW BUS OFFICES. THE PILLAR IS A PORTION OF THE RENAISSANCE STRUCTURE WHICH SUPERSEDED THE MEDIEVAL CROSS AT THE TOWN CENTRE; A CROSS MARKED IN THE ROADWAY INDICATES ITS SITE acquire worldly accomplishments but were obliged to receive instruction in toning and psalmody and the principles of religion. In 1771 the Leicester Infirmary was built by public subscription and became at once the town's most widely supported charitable institution. The inception and success of the scheme were largely due to Dr. William Watts, a modest physician and clergyman who consistently neglected chances of contemporary preferment for the humble life of a curate and for opportunities to benefit his neighbours and their posterity.

A further contribution to public improvements came from the individual parishes which were still charged with a great many functions that later became municipal or national. The most important of these was the care of the poor: St. Martin's vestry in particular has preserved valuable records of its activities in this respect which included the erection and maintenance of a workhouse.

The eighteenth century had coped, more or less adequately, with a population which rose from about 6,000 to over 17,000. The old timber houses had been rebuilt, one at a time, in brick. Because of the numerous separate freeholds and because the old street-lines had been mainly retained there was then no planned lay-out of crescents or squares such as add elegance to some other towns. Because there was still plenty of room, most of the larger houses were not typically urban, but stood detached in their own grounds, a fact which was unfortunately to ensure their demolition before they were old enough to be valued for their architecture or remembered for their associations. (When they pulled down the old mansion that had belonged in turn to a Herrick, a Noble, a Pares, and a Burnaby, the area reverted to the old name of the Grey Friars. Perhaps the ghost of a not-so-famous man, a certain Mr. Pocklington[1] consoles himself as he paces what was once his favourite garden Walk by murmuring, 'And some there be which have *no* memorial'.)

The physical appearance of such a rapidly changing town is not very easy to visualize. If a Tudor citizen could have revisited Leicester towards the end of the eighteenth century he would have been impressed by its growth, by the broad, paved streets and by the great number and regular proportions of the brick buildings. He would have remarked that what he knew as High Street was now called Highcross Street, that what he had called Swinemarket was now High Street and that the actual swine-market had moved to Bond Street. He would specially have noticed that the centre of the town had moved eastwards and that the principal inns were outside the line of the old walls. It would have seemed to him, altogether, a much overgrown but a busy, orderly place,

---

[1] Was he, perhaps the John Pocklington who was Mayor in 1778 but who 'in 1789 only paid eleven and threepence in the pound on a debt of £20 due to Trinity Hospital and died a poor man, a pensioner of the corporation'? (R. W. Greaves *The Corporation of Leicester* 1689-1836, p. 13.)

cut off from the country in a new way by something less tangible but more potent than walls.

An aristocratic tourist in 1789 noted, indeed, that the town, owing to 'manufactories' had grown so much that a plan of 1610 which he possessed was a curiosity. He found the streets wide, the market place gay and spacious and the Three Cranes Inn excellent. But the houses were not impressive and the coffee house (where it was a convenience to find that the mail coach now brought the previous day's London papers) was a very bad one. And he qualified even his praise by reflecting that 'after all a good country inn makes but a bad London tavern, as a good street of a country town would make but a paltry figure in London'.[1]

In William Gardiner's *Music and Friends,* Leicester at the end of the eighteenth century is viewed from yet another angle. As he thought of his childhood he was chiefly impressed by the town's still rural aspect at that time. He remembered especially the trees—two great elms near the Borough Gaol in Highcross Street whose branches met across the street, a very tall holly near Blue Boar Lane and a row of massive chestnut trees 'hiding some wretched buildings' somewhere near Southgate Street. 'In the Market Place was the Pigeon Tree, under which the country-women sat to sell pigeons, a great article of food brought from the open corn-fields that surrounded Leicester in all directions. Opposite the Post Office (in Granby Street) there was a grove of trees under which stood the small thatched inn called the "Jolly Miller".'

If any impression of the appearance of the town varies according to what aspects are emphasized, so does any impression of the life that was lived there. The difference between that of the upper and that of the lower classes was enormous. It was not merely, as it was in the next century, a difference that could be expressed in terms of solid material comfort. The well-born and wealthy still had much more than that. When Charles Winstanley, Esq., was chosen for the shrievalty in 1774 he was attended by 'four hundred horsemen headed by thirty gentlemen in blue uniforms with crimson collars and white breeches'. In the same year (it was the year the town gates were taken down) the Infirmary Anniversary was celebrated by a choral service at St. Martin's, a banquet at the Town Hall, a grand concert at the Castle and, in St. Martin's the next morning, an oratorio. The brilliant company included, besides all the local nobility, Lord Sandwich who 'appeared in the orchestra and played the kettledrums, and assisted with part of his own band' and Mr. Banks with Omai, prince of Otaheite, 'who had been brought to this country by Captain Cooke, the celebrated circumnavigator'. At about the same time the unenlightened workpeople were earning (the better

[1] *The Torrington Diaries*: Containing the tours through England and Wales of the Hon. John Byng (afterwards fifth Viscount Torrington) between the years 1781 and 1794. Edited by C. Bruyn Andrews, London: Eyre and Spottiswoode (Publishers) Ltd., 1935. Vol. II, *A Tour in the Midlands* 1789. (The diarist spent several days in Leicester and his account of the antiquities then visible is interesting though superficial.)

class of them) about 7s. 3d. a week in summer and 6s. 6d. in winter after paying for frame-rent and candles. It is hardly surprising that they were so incapable of taking long views that in 1773 they made 'an indefensible attack upon the rights of property' by destroying an improved stocking-frame which they believed would result in the employment of fewer men at less wages. More serious riots occurred in 1787 when a mob broke up Mr. Whetstone's new worsted spinning machinery, tried to storm Mr. Whetstone's house and stoned the Mayor who actually died of an injury he received. Seven years later, when the price of wheat went to £8 a quarter (a price which may be compared with the 'standard' price of 45s. in the 1932 Wheat Act) there were bread riots culminating in the 'Barrow Butchery' in which the Leicester Troop of Cavalry killed or badly wounded eleven men out of a mob trying to seize a wagon of wheat. In this year the Leicester races were abandoned—a gesture both of prudence and of decency.

Nobody in particular was to blame. The only possible solutions of England's population problem were starvation, emigration, or the export of manufactured goods; and it was more than fifty years before the adoption of the last course proved successful enough to give the workers themselves more than the barest subsistence. What is perhaps more important, nobody, except actual rioters, was generally held blameworthy at the time. The gentry were doing no harm, and giving some pleasure, by riding about in blue uniforms, patronizing musicians, supporting the infirmary and spending their money locally. The manufacturers were paying as good wages as they could afford to as many people as they could employ. People who were well off did their best to relieve acute distress. On one occasion a Mr. Alderman Phipps brought a ton of salted butter from Ireland and retailed it at prime cost; on another a fund of £400 was raised to sell bread at half price and coals at 4d. per hundred. One's particular sympathies go out to the committee who in 1796 made large purchases of corn in distant markets to provide against threatened famine and who in consequence of an unexpectedly good (and presumably early) harvest were left with stocks on their hands which they had to sell in the county at a loss of £1,550.

The workers themselves were on the whole patient and at the worst misguided. Whether they were quite as misguided as they seemed to contemporaries may possibly be questioned. It was considered a dreadful thing that by breaking Mr. Whetstone's machine they delayed the introduction of worsted spinning mills to Leicester for twenty years, but in fact there was an adequate supply of cheap hand-spun wool available locally and as soon as it became necessary for hosiers to buy yarn from a distance, spinning mills were set up without opposition.[1]

[1] The idea that it was a social duty to exploit any invention immediately and to the full was quite a new one. William Lee had invented the stocking-frame in 1589, a hundred years before its use became general.

If one must seek for a scapegoat, there is, of course, the stock figure of the Old Corporation. Had its leaders been abler and wiser they might possibly have used their power to extend the parliamentary franchise[1] as a weapon to exert control over labour conditions, though they could not have done anything to raise general wage levels. But the belated, half-hearted and ultimately tragic intervention of the mayor in the riot of 1787 ('Come, my lads, give over—you've done enough—quite enough: come, give over, there's good lads, and go away') was an epitome of their unfortunate history.

By the end of the century the chance of any mediation from that quarter had been lost. Men of property, whether Tories or progressives, were huddled together in an uneasy alliance against anything that looked like a spread of revolutionary doctrine from across the Channel. In 1778, reckless, generous Charles Rozzel[2] had conjured the workmen to 'exercise the rights which nature and the constitution had given you' but his fiery talent was burnt out or quenched, and when the respectable and afterwards eminent bookseller Richard Phillips had been imprisoned on a doubtful charge of selling *The Rights of Man,* no one ventured to say much more about the rights of framework-knitters.

It is pleasanter to turn to another form of progress that did no material harm to anyone and much material good to the whole community in Leicester. A corollary of the growth of national and international trade was a need for improved communications. First the turnpike roads were developed. By 1764 it was possible (in a vehicle known as 'The Flying Machine') to leave Leicester at two in the morning and reach London the same night. Two years later the service was extended to Manchester and from this time Leicester's position in the middle of England began to be more of an advantage than a hindrance to her trade. Canals came next, relieving an acute fuel shortage by bringing cheap coal from Derbyshire; and finally the Railway Age opened when in 1832 the Leicester and Swannington Railway, notable for the longest tunnel in England, triumphantly carried Leicestershire coal round the age-old barrier of the Charnwood Forest.

The seal was dramatically set on Leicester's achievements in this field when one of her citizens, Thomas Cook, organized the first excursion

---

[1] 'The Leicester franchise was . . . extended to include all freemen not receiving alms and householders paying scot and lot. This democratic ruling, however, did not destroy (though it limited) the influence of the oligarchical corporation, since it had been held by the courts from the seventeenth century that corporations might with perfect legality make anybody free, irrespective of residence, if only for the purpose of creating a vote for an election.'—R. W. Greaves, *The Corporation of Leicester*, 1689-1836, p. 88.

[2] Charles Rozzel, a brilliant but unstable young man, raised himself from a humble position, learned Greek and Latin, and might, with a better start, have become a considerable writer of some sort. He was secretary and laureate of the Whig 'Revolution Club'. There is an affectionate notice of him in Throsby's *Leicester*—for a disparaging account see *The Torrington Diary*.

train in 1841. It only ran from Leicester to Loughborough but it blazed the beginning of a long trail.

By the time the railways were in being, the opening of new markets had brought the hosiery trade an accession of vigour if not yet of prosperity. Though the conditions of the workmen were little if any better, they were prepared to sink their difference with the masters and join them in attacking what seemed a common enemy. One grievance at least they could share: they had rights of which they felt unjustly deprived. And although their ideas as to who should have what rights were as different as their chances of getting them, although when it came to the point the demands of Thomas Cooper and the Chartists were as stoutly resisted by Liberal manufacturers as by anyone else of the propertied classes, it seemed, and probably was, a step in the right direction for the workers when the exclusive rights and privileges of the Old Corporation were got rid of. Few if any manual workers obtained the parliamentary franchise and though they did, if they were ratepayers, get a municipal vote, they were still a ridiculously long way from any chance of electing actual representatives of their own class or interests; but the cheering was loud enough to drown any grumbling voices. In a ruder age they would undoubtedly have celebrated the occasion by hanging the town clerk; in 1836 it seemed more feasible, if less satisfactory, to have the civic regalia and town plate sold by auction, presumably in the expectation that aldermen and councillors would never again walk in procession or dine at the public expense.

There was another bond which many masters and many men had in common and which helped to divide them from what they had both come to regard as the privileged classes. They were, for various reasons and in various ways, Dissenters, or, as they were now more often called, Nonconformists. Wesley's addresses in the great barn near Grey Friars or in the Castle-yard[1] had brought a message of hope in Heaven if not on earth to many poor wretches who, if they could have gained admittance, would have listened unmoved to the 'rational manly and devout' sermon which so pleased the distinguished company in St. Martin's Church at the Infirmary Anniversary. Other and older sects had each a special contribution to make. The Baptist ministry produced two outstanding men, Robert Hall, a preacher of national fame, and William Carey, a saintly missionary and a notable Oriental scholar. Throughout the Victorian age, Unitarians of the Great Meeting were among the intellectual leaders of the town. It was characteristic of their approach to the problems of the time that they organized and financed a Domestic Mission whose leader, Joseph Dare, not only gave a life of personal service to the poorest classes of the community but, through his annual

---

[1] 'In the evening I preached in the Castle-yard at Leicester, to a multitude of awakened and unawakened. One feeble attempt was made to disturb them: a man was sent to cry fresh salmon at a little distance; but he might as well have spared his pains, for none took the least notice of him'. *Wesley's Journal*, 31 July, 1770.

reports, made it impossible for comfortable people to ignore the existence of social conditions which could not, in conscience, be tolerated. The Society of Friends were neither a numerous nor a proselytizing body but, somehow, there was generally one of their number to the fore when a piece of practical philanthropy was needed. It was a Quaker who, when the Chimney Sweeps Act was passed, gave every master-sweep in Leicester a good dinner and a set of long-handled brushes— and then told them that as a magistrate he would henceforward show no mercy to any one of them who was found putting a boy up a chimney.

The list could be extended and the examples multiplied. The essential point is, however, that every congregation worked as a team and each in a slightly different way. Chapel membership meant a good deal more than a common opinion on points of doctrine or church government: the loyalties and obligations that were implied brought back a good deal of the spirit of the old religious gilds.

It was fortunate for Leicester that the Church of England, unlike the Old Corporation, responded to the challenge by setting its own house in order before it was too late. Churches were built and endowed to serve new working-class parishes and it was a member of a notable clerical family, associated with St. Martin's for eighty years, who founded in 1862 the Vaughan Working Men's College.

It remained unfortunately true that Nonconformity and the Establishment were seldom able to work together in harmony for a common cause. In 1835 the proposal to found a single first-class school in Leicester broke down for this reason and two separate institutions, the Collegiate School and the Proprietary School, both failed after a few years for lack of adequate support. In other fields, rival societies entailed duplication of effort, if not a diminution of results. It is satisfactory to record, however, that one institution, the Literary and Philosophical Society, provided neutral ground where Tories and Radicals listened to one another's learned discourses and where Churchmen and Dissenters were united in the pursuit of knowledge and the defence of culture.

In 1849 the Society formally presented to the town the collection that formed the nucleus of the Leicester Museum—a transaction that has proved as satisfactory as it was creditable to both donors and recipients.

If one slips, perhaps too easily, into writing of nineteenth century Leicester in terms of middle-class activities, it is because the middle classes were dominant, and in a new way. Not only had they regained control of the town's internal affairs, but they had ceased to defer to any superior class or dignitary in those of the nation. Socially they still did so but with a rather bad grace and as it became easier and pleasanter for county society to go to London instead of the county town when they were not visiting one another's houses or having it all their own way (a rather wild and wicked way some Leicester people thought) in a cosy little town like Melton, prominent burgesses and their wives were less and less often embarrassed by the necessity of acknowledging an alien leadership in charitable enterprises or yielding precedence at local balls.

There was, it must be admitted, a good deal of loss in this. Leicester had been, for the first quarter of the century, a minor musical centre under the leadership of the county gentleman Joseph Cradock and the middle-class enthusiast William Gardiner. It was so no longer. Hardworking, self-educated men were willing to devote their spare time to religious activities, to improving other people's lives and their own minds. The arts, if they were not eschewed as dangerous, might, in their more distant and respectable manifestations, be saluted with distant respect. They were still practised—by professionals and young women; buildings were decorated, furniture and pictures produced, plays acted, pianos strummed, songs sung. But the traditions of critical appreciation and enjoyment had gone with the leisured classes and if such things were by no means always done badly there was no sufficient incentive to do them always well.

The greatest loss fell on the Victorians themselves and we have no reason to complain very bitterly of the legacy they left us. They were faced with a great many tremendous tasks and they accomplished most of them. The basic business of earning a living—let alone a fortune— was not as easy as it seems in retrospect. In the first half of the century, whilst markets were being painfully conquered, the hosiery industry knew long periods of depression which brought owners near to bankruptcy and framework-knitters very near indeed to starvation. Just when things might have been expected to look up a little, the possibility of using steam engines instead of human power reduced, for the time being, the number and changed the kind of workers needed. Riots—partly political but basically a protest against intolerable conditions—did no good to anybody.

Things very nearly took a very ugly turn in 1842 when about 1,500 Chartists armed with stones and bludgeons were charged and dispersed by the police and Yeomanry but fortunately 'The Battle of Mowmacre Hill' produced no serious casualties and was remembered in the best possible way, as a joke against both sides.[1]

Though there were even more serious riots in 1848, trade suddenly improved in 1849 and the corner was definitely turned in 1853 when Thomas Crick invented in Leicester the hand-riveted, as opposed to the hand-sewn, boot. The new craft spread rapidly: it was exactly what was wanted because it could absorb surplus male labour whilst the new hosiery factories were finding occupation for the women and girls. No doubt also the trade was easier to establish because in the early days the work was, like hosiery-knitting, 'put out' to be done in all sorts of

[1] It is said that there was one casualty, of a sort, during a night patrol of the streets— I hope the veterans of two major wars will forgive me for disinterring it. Within living memory, if one of the Yeomanry Cavalry walked through Leicester in uniform, he was liable to be pursued by the inquiry, 'Who shot the pump?'

back rooms and sheds—though from other points of view this was by no means an ideal arrangement. It was a curious and fortunate coincidence that elastic-sided boots came into fashion just then and that the manufacture of elastic webbing was already established in Leicester as a branch of the hosiery industry.

After this, Leicester could fairly claim to have established a satisfactory and stable basis for its economic life. It was no longer entirely dependent on the prosperity of a single trade and became still less so when the boot and hosiery industries were supplemented by light engineering and other manufacturing trades which depended more on a supply of good-class labour than on local raw materials. The changeover from home employment to factory labour came late enough for factories to be built and equipped to provide decent working conditions. The facts that power requirements were not heavy and that Leicester had been one of the first towns to implement the Smoke Abatement Act minimized the amount of smoke and dirt involved. Leicester's fortunate position, as seen by her own spokesmen in the early 'seventies, was summarized as follows in *Spencer's Handy Guide:*

> Few towns of the same size make such a display of costly buildings for trade purposes; these reflect the liberal spirit of their proprietors, who by setting before us these 'things of beauty' ennoble their town and soften the asperity of a life of toil, giving the luxuries of pleasing forms and colours, free space, and pure air, even to the work-room and the counting house. Men of lower and narrower views may condemn this profuse expenditure upon what they would call 'dead stock'; but without more than a passing allusion to the benevolence which promotes the workers' happiness for its own sake, there is a motive which must satisfy even 'business-men'. One venerable proprietor, belonging to that large class who have ascended from the base to the summit of our social fabric, informed us that he found it *to his interest* to maintain his workpeople in the highest possible health and vigour. Another remarked that in the close crowded rooms of his old factories the young women used often to faint at their work, but that such hindrances never occur in the noble mansion which he has lately erected for their use.

If this sounds, nowadays, rather crude—indeed rather horribly like an extract from *Uncle Tom's Cabin*—it at least indicates that benevolence, enlightened self-interest, and a desire to advertise their own prosperity had combined to induce many Leicester manufacturers to set a standard very much higher than the minimum which factory legislation and inspection were beginning to require.

If the satisfactory solution of economic difficulties and to a very large extent the conditions of factory work were still left to individual initiative, there were other pressing problems which could only be solved by corporate effort. A population which rose from 17,000 to 219,000 during the century not only had to be clothed, fed, and housed, it also had to be provided with water, sanitation, transport, and if possible schools, hospitals and open spaces as well as, unfortunately, workhouses, asylums and prisons.

Water was the fundamental and most difficult problem. Old Leicester had stood on a little rising ground near the river. New Leicester spread over a basin surrounded by hills, but they were hills with no considerable springs. The river itself was in every way a nuisance. It was not fit to drink, it flooded the houses every year, and it was neither big enough nor sufficiently below the level of the town to carry off the sewage.

To provide clean water, Thornton reservoir was made in 1853, Cropston in 1866, Swithland in 1894. Each scheme was thought (by those with good wells of their own) extravagant and overbold; each in turn proved inadequate; though Leicester has gone much farther since, adequate water supply in periods of low rainfall can still cause some problems.

For sewage, a pumping and drying station was erected near the Abbey. It was fondly hoped that the sale of the dried material would prove very profitable till it was found that the valuable manurial salts were all carried off in the water. A long respite was gained, however, when in the 'eighties a large area of land was acquired at Beaumont Leys. This acquisition has proved a boon in the later half of the twentieth century as the Beaumont Leys area provides the site for a major housing development, almost amounting to a satellite town.

Floods were mastered, after much tinkering, by blowing up a number of obstructive mills and straightening the course of the river.

Finally, after very many miles of sewers had been laid, after those which silted up had been reopened and cleansed, after most of the drains which economical builders had omitted to connect with the sewers had been discovered and rectified, the death-rate began to fall again and Leicester gradually changed from a most unhealthy to a fairly healthy town—it was not till after the end of the nineteenth century that 'very' could be substituted for 'fairly'.

There would be no point in detailing everything else that was done, and how and when. Most of the Council's tasks were common to all English municipalities and the results of their labours are still there to be seen. Two points, perhaps, are worth making.

The first is that, in Leicester at any rate, municipal action was both assisted and anticipated, particularly in the educational and cultural fields, by voluntary effort or individual munificence. To take two examples from among many, the Bishop Street Library was given by Andrew Carnegie and erected on a site provided by the Corporation; the Art Gallery was founded by public subscription but responsibility for its maintenance and housing was assumed by the town.

The second point is that in undertaking municipal enterprises the Liberal majority were breaking with the narrow tradition in which they had been brought up, and must be given the more credit on that account.

Their doctrine, in its purest form, laid it down that if anything was needed by the community, the community would be prepared to pay for it and private enterprise would find it profitable to supply the need. But when they found that in municipal affairs this doctrine did not always work out satisfactorily—either that people would die before private enterprise could be sure of a dividend or that where a monopoly was inevitable the reward to private enterprise might be disproportionately great—they had the courage to say, 'So much the worse for the doctrine' and take the action that seemed good to them. If they fell short, according to our ideas, in some respects, it was because they were obliged, both by their own instincts and by their need for support from their party, to compromise heavily. They stopped short as soon as they had reached the point where private enterprise could carry on, and every time they widened a road or drained a swamp they put money into the pockets of the thoughtful and well-informed people who had acquired land which would presently be ripe for development. One may regret that more of the profit did not come back to the ratepayers, or, alternatively, that people were not prohibited from building on land that was known to flood,[1] but probably the line that was taken was the only means then available of getting things done somehow and done quickly.

Somehow, and quickly, the new Leicester got itself built. It was very different from the old Leicester. Belgrave Gate and Gallowtree Gate, once a by-pass road outside the walls, convenient in time of plague, had suffered the usual fate of by-passes in becoming a central and congested thoroughfare. Mansions in the country like Westcotes and Dannett's (or Danet's) Hall had followed spacious town houses to destruction and an oblivion hardly mitigated by the naming of a mean or middle-class street. Their successors were the large Victorian houses spaced at intervals along the London road beyond what was in turn called the New Racecourse, the Racecourse, the Old Racecourse, and finally the Victoria Park. At the other end of the town a bold, early, and much criticized venture had been the laying out of the Abbey Park on a piece of marshy ground in a poor district.[2] All the while, as new houses were put up, less convenient but more picturesque parts of the old town were being pulled down, streets widened and markets moved, not without indignant clamour, to new sites.

In every respect the new Leicester was (at the end of the nineteenth century) a compromise. It was a compromise between planning and

---

[1] A writer in *Leicestershire Notes and Queries* (1893) could remember 'the ground between the West Bridge and the late Grass Weir near the Braunstone Gate Bridge (now all built over) being a swampy field that a horse could not cross at midsummer. Horses were sometimes put there to pasture, but a pair of gears was always kept purposely that when a horse got bogged it might be possible to extricate it'.

[2] 'Perhaps it would be rash as yet to designate the coming Abbey Meadow Park "Our Corporation Folly," but the very large expenditure going on and contemplated in that dank, diphtherial and febrile spot, positively gives me the shivers'.—*Modern Leicester*, by Robert Read, Junior, 1881.

haphazard development, a compromise between the desire to start fresh and the desire to retain old associations, a compromise between Philistinism and culture, a compromise between manufacturing and agricultural interests. And if no compromise is wholly to anybody's liking—well, there had been one ugly reminder in Leicester that the worst scandals may happen, not when somebody finds an opportunity to feather his nest, not when some obstinate fellow is, with a tolerant shrug, allowed to hold up progress by his sentimental attachment to something useless and out of date, but when representatives and officials are given a free hand to carry out a doctrinaire policy to its logical conclusion. Nothing was ever so modern, so up to date, so highly approved by penal reformers, as the new County Gaol, put up in 1828 and arranged for the celebrated 'separate system'. It had treadmills, it had straight waistcoats, it had cranks—and in 1854 England learned with horror from the report of a Royal Commission that the good intentions of magistrates had paved the way to a Hell on earth.[1]

By 1900 or thereabouts, that particular episode may have been forgotten but the moral to which it had pointed was generally recognized. Party feeling ran high enough at General Elections, and was to run higher yet, but in the affairs of their own town, people were I think becoming a good deal more inclined to look at cases on their merits than to refer them to the test of a preconceived doctrine—provided, that is, that the point under discussion had no close bearing on the merits of the Boer War, Free Trade, Home Rule, Temperance, or Women's Rights.

But with the turn of the century, historical reconstruction begins to give place to perhaps even more fallible personal memories, and the controversies of the years that followed are not yet safely dead. The great surge forward in population and production that had begun in the eighteenth century and had gathered strength in the nineteenth was slowing down, perhaps to consolidate for another advance, perhaps not. The historian of the future may think fit to begin a new chapter with the election of 1906 or with the War of 1914 or with the peace of 1945. Let us, however, for the present, leave Leicester as some of us first remember it, prosperous, self-confident, high- and a little narrow-minded, more often described by strangers as a clean than as a beautiful town. The last generation of horses were pulling the trams and the buses, the last of the last generation of framework-knitters were still plying their craft. The Midland Railway had a new and admired station on the London Road; the Great Central line had just been completed. The High Street was being widened; this and the clearance of a new way through the Newarke would, it was believed, solve for ever Leicester's worst traffic problems. The old banking firm of Pares were putting up a new building

---

[1] Those who are interested to know the facts can learn them from *English Prisons under Local Government,* by Beatrice and Sidney Webb, or, in substance, from Charles Reade's novel *It's Never Too Late to Mend,* the prison chapters of which were closely based on the Reports on the Leicester and Birmingham prisons.

in St. Martins which was only to bear their name for a few months before it became Parr's Bank. Twenty years later the bank became the Westminster, and subsequently the National Westminster, but throughout these changes of name, the building remains an enduring monument to the skill of their architect, Perkins Pick. Near the Clock Tower, P.C. Stephens was on duty; in him, it seemed to us, Leicester had quite as notable a representative of law and order as when Daniel Lambert was the town gaoler.

Whether, at that time, we admired Leicester critically or uncritically, or did not admire it at all, it was our own and we were learning to value its traditions. Mrs. Fielding Johnson had published her charming book *Glimpses of Ancient Leicester* in 1891 and those of us who were lucky were brought up on it. In 1906 she brought out a second edition and we may note that in revising a list of contemporary phenomena she deleted 'tramcars and tricycles' and substituted 'electric or motor cars, bicycles, and perambulators'.[1] At the end, she mentioned some former antiquaries and historians, adding, 'May it not be reasonably hoped that the same interest in the past life of Leicester will be continued among its present citizens and handed on, together with a practical desire to improve its conditions and to beautify its aspects, to future generations of dwellers in this ancient town'. That sentence, after seventy years, needs no revision.

FURTHER INFORMATION

The History of Leicester in the Eighteenth Century, by James Thompson (1870), based on Borough records and, apparently, on a search of newspaper files, gives a good and full account of the facts, interpreted with a bias in favour of nineteenth century Liberalism.

Throsby's History of Leicester contains a good deal of interesting contemporary information and anecdotage, including characters of recently deceased citizens.

The Rev. Samuel Carte, at the beginning of the eighteenth century, wrote a good deal on antiquarian matters. A part of his MS. is reprinted in Nichols: the original is in the Bodleian.

Music and Friends, by William Gardiner, is a discursive and readable autobiography; the author lived from 1770 to 1853.

The Memoirs of Joseph Cradock, of Gumley, is an interesting book of the same period and also largely concerned with musical matters.

The Corporation of Leicester, 1689-1836, by R. W. Greaves, is a short, well-written, and scholarly modern book (2nd edition 1970).

Records of the Borough of Leicester, Vol. V Hall Books and Papers 1689-1835, edited by G. A. Chinnery—provides an invaluable source for the history of the earlier part of this period.

[1] Perambulators were certainly invented before 1891, but I think they did not become popular until smooth sidewalks of gravel or flat concrete slabs replaced the 'kidney stones.' Old-fashioned people maintained that 'the shaking was bad for the spine'.

Radical Leicester: a history of Leicester 1780-1850, by A. T. Patterson (University College, Leicester): A complete account of many aspects of reform in the period. The history of Trade Union movements is well dealt with.

The second edition (1906) of Mrs. Fielding Johnson's *Glimpses of Ancient Leicester* includes an account of the first half of the nineteenth century which is informative and valuable.

A Historical Sketch, by J. Storey, a former town clerk, is a useful reference book, giving the dates of various municipal undertakings.

Nineteenth Century Leicester, by I. C. Ellis, includes a large number of anecdotes and sketches of personalities, mainly of the second half of the century.

The Centenary Book of the Leicester Literary and Philosophical Society, by F. B. Lott, and the *Transactions* of the Society give a picture of one important aspect of Leicester life.

A Leicestershire Road, by Percy Russell, contains a great deal of interesting information about conditions of transport in the eighteenth and nineteenth centuries and of the operations of the turnpike trust.

Most of the material for the history of nineteenth century Leicester must, however, be sought in guides, directories, municipal records and accounts, in the published or unpublished records of commercial firms and in the files of the local newspapers.

DATES FOR REFERENCE

General History		Leicester	
A.D.		A.D.	
1702	Accession of Queen Anne	1708	Move to enclose South Fields
1714	Accession of George I		
1727	Accession of George II		
1745	Young Pretender's Rebellion		
		1749	Non-freemen win case against attempted restrictions by Corporation
			First street lighting
		1759	Public pumps erected
1760	Accession of George III		
		1764	'Flying Machine' coach does journey from Leicester to London in the day
			Provision riots
		1767	Infirmary established
		1774	Town Gates taken down
1776	American Independence		
		1784	Severe winter and much distress
		1785	New Walk laid out
			Howard visits prisons and Infirmary
		1787	Spinning machines destroyed
1789	French Revolution		
1793	War with France	1793	Richard Phillips imprisoned for selling *The Rights of Man*

General History	Leicester
A.D.	A.D.
	1794 Loughborough canal opened
	1795 Corn famine: the 'Barrow Butchery'
	1800 Assembly Rooms opened
	1808 'More than 50 stage coaches pass through Leicester daily'
	1812 Distress among framework-knitters
1815 Waterloo	
1820 Accession of George IV	
	1821 Gas lamps introduced in the streets
1829 Catholic Emancipation	
1830 Accession of William IV	
1832 Reform Bill	1832 Leicester and Swannington Railway opened
1834 Poor Law Amendment Act	
1835 Municipal Reform Act	1835 Literary and Philosophical Society founded
	End of Old Corporation
	Town Council elected with Liberal majority (Dec. 26)
1837 Accession of Queen Victoria	
	1842 Chartist riots. 'Battle of Mowmacre Hill'
	1843 Visit of Queen Victoria, Prince Albert, and Duke of Wellington, who travelled in private carriages on railway trucks
1846 Corn Laws repealed	
1848 Chartist Demonstration	1848 Rioting in Leicester
	1849 Town Museum opened
1850 More stringent Factory Regulations	
1853 Crimean War	1853 Water brought from Thornton Reservoir
1857 Indian Mutiny	
1861 American Civil War	
1870 Elementary Education Act	1870 Free Library opened
	1871 Flood schemes begun
1874 Income Tax 2d. in the £	1874 Belgrave Road horse trams started
	1876 New Town Hall opened
	1877 Wyggeston Boys' School opened
	1882 Opening of Abbey Park by Prince and Princess of Wales
	1883 Highcross Street market moved to Market Place

	General History		Leicester
A.D.		A.D.	
		1885	Opening of Art Gallery
1886	First Home Rule Bill		
1887	Jubilee		
		1891	Extension of Borough
1897	Diamond Jubilee		
		1898	Derwent Water Undertaking inaugurated
1899	Boer War		
1901	Death of Queen Victoria		

POPULATION OF LEICESTER

1562	about	4,000
1700	,,	6,000
1800	,,	17,000[1]
1845		54,000
1850		59,000
1860		67,000
1870		92,000
1880		120,000
1890		154,000
1900		219,000

[1] Census figures begin in 1801.

Section II

EIGHTEENTH AND NINETEENTH CENTURY BUILDINGS

THE great majority of the buildings now standing in Leicester belong to the second half of the nineteenth or to the twentieth century but there remain just—and only just—enough examples of those erected between 1700 and 1850 to illustrate the history of architecture and life in Leicester during that period in all its changing phases. Moreover, so many of these buildings are now the property of either the City Council or the County Council that these bodies can claim chief credit for the existence of this position and would, on the other hand, bear the heaviest responsibility if it were not maintained.

The list which follows is not exhaustive and anyone who walks about Leicester with his eyes open may find interest in adding to it. As a rough guide to the age of buildings, it may be said that the use of narrow bricks usually indicates eighteenth century work and stucco the period 1820-50. Houses and cottages roofed with Swithland slates were probably not built much later than 1850.

With the exception of the group of houses at Belgrave, only buildings that were *originally* urban or at least suburban have been included. The

111

villages of Knighton, Aylestone, Braunstone, Humberstone, and Evington, inside the present City, contain enough interesting buildings (beside their churches) to warrant a separate study which would be out of place here.

I must add two cautionary notes. One is that the dates given for buildings in various books I have consulted do not always agree to a year, partly, no doubt, because buildings were often planned in one year, started in another and finished in another. It seemed, however, unnecessarily cumbersome to say 'about' in each case: what is really important is to know the period to which a building belongs.

The other point that must be remembered is that very few buildings (of this or any other period) have remained completely unaltered since they were built. In a brief review like this it is impossible to trace the complete history of such alterations and I have not attempted to do so when the general appearance of a building still conforms to the original conception.

THE EIGHTEENTH CENTURY

THE CASTLE AND CASTLE HOUSE

Although, as noted in previous sections, some of its structure dates back to Norman times, the Castle was refronted at the beginning of the eighteenth century and it is in outward appearance a dignified Queen Anne brick building. Castle House, just outside the north entrance of the courtyard, is mid-eighteenth century and is our only example of a Georgian house in the town itself which does not form part of a continuous street-frontage.

BELGRAVE HALL CROSS CORNERS BELGRAVE HOUSE

The leadwork on the Hall bears the dates 1709 and 1713. The style of the building, however, suggests that it may be earlier. The stable block which is in more orthodox classical style has the date 1710 worked into the brickwork. Cross Corners, part of the same property and perhaps at one time a dower house, appears to be later eighteenth century work, and Belgrave House, nearly opposite the Hall, is probably later still. Belgrave Hall is furnished as a period museum and the house and gardens are open to the public (10 a.m. to 5.30 p.m. on weekdays and 2 p.m. to 5.30 p.m. on Sundays, throughout the year).

THE GREAT MEETING (BOND STREET)

The very plain brick hall, built in 1708, has been enlarged, but most of the original work remains. In the graveyard there is an interesting series of Swithland slate tombstones which show very well the progressive elaboration of lettering and ornament that went on during the Georgian period and the sudden revulsion of taste that occurred soon after 1820.

ST. MARTIN'S NEW STREET AND FRIAR LANE

No. 21 St. Martins (in use by the nearby school) is a charming and well-cared for eighteenth century urban gentleman's house. Facing the cathedral is what was once an excellent example of a block of good houses designed

(continued on page 114)

THE CLOCKTOWER, 1868: TYPICAL OF THE GOTHIC REVIVAL. PHOTOGRAPHED IN 1968

ARCHITECTURAL EVIDENCE OF HISTORY IN
THE CITY CENTRE
Based on the plan by Hugh Collinson

KEY TO THE BUILDINGS SHOWN OPPOSITE

as a whole, but one projecting wing has evidently been shorn off and the front rebuilt in alignment with the street. There are some other good eighteenth century houses in St. Martin's East.

New Street, in spite of a few new buildings, retains as a whole the character of the eighteenth century in which it was laid out. In Friar Lane 'Dr. Benfield's House' presents a superb example of a decorated classical façade and some of the other houses are contemporary.

HIGHCROSS STREET
AND
SOUTHGATE STREET

Although here and there a good door and fan-light or the upper part of a façade indicates what was once a dignified dwelling-house, the best, and certainly the best preserved reminder of what this quarter was like at the end of the eighteenth century is the former 18 Highcross Street, the fine façade of which was added in 1796 to a much older house ('Roger Wygston's House' noted in Part III, Section II). The whole building has recently been restored and opened as a Costume Museum.

THE NEWARKE

Until well on in the nineteenth century, the Newarke was a select residential quarter and contained at least half a dozen fine town houses. Most of these are gone, but the façade of the Gateway School is an outstanding example of how, sometimes, an architectural treasure can be preserved to dignify buildings with another function. It is perhaps worth noting that the tiny projecting wing built on to the older Newarke Houses is just the sort of stucco 'Gothick' toy that Horace Walpole and a few other cultivated people at the end of the eighteenth century used to make for their own amusement.

A FACTORY

Probably the oldest factory building in Leicester is that of Donisthorpe & Co. in Sarah Street (but most easily visible from the Canal Towpath) which is a characteristic Georgian building.

THE COUNTY
ROOMS

The 'Assembly Rooms', as they are still sometimes called, were erected about 1792 to the designs of John Johnson, an architect whose other claim to remembrance was his foundation of a charity known as 'The Consanguinitarium' for those of his kin who were in poor circumstances. Its rooms have the lightness and grace that we associate with the Regency. The stone of the façade unfortunately suffered the fate, unusual in Leicester, of severe blackening which obscured the gaiety of the intention, but modern methods of cleaning have remedied this for the time being at least.

THE EARLY NINETEENTH CENTURY

A CHAPEL

Bishop Street (Methodist) Chapel (1815), a brick building in the classical tradition, achieves something more than the sober respectability which was presumably aimed at. It has the quiet distinction of a man wearing a plain but extremely well-cut suit and is well worthy of one of the best sites in the city.

114

H.M. PRISON

The architect of what was then the new County Gaol (1828) also turned to the Middle Ages for inspiration. He did not aim at beauty and was successful in implying strength—though unless, as is possible, he was remembering the storming of the Bastille, it is difficult to see why he concentrated on showing that it would be exceedingly difficult for malefactors to get *into* the building without permission.

THE CENTRAL LENDING LIBRARY

This building, erected in 1831, is, on the other hand, in the severest and plainest version of the classical style, using the newly popular stucco. It is saved from ugliness by its good proportions. These have not been destroyed by the recent careful alterations, which, externally, consist of a raising of the lower windows and the addition of a porch. (The building was originally put up by a company for accommodating public meetings and part of it housed the Mechanics' Institute for some years.)

UNIVERSITY

Some of the last good classical buildings in England are those in which no money was spared for ornament, notably the workhouses of the New Poor Law. The central block of the University was erected in 1836 as a lunatic asylum. The materials used were obviously the cheapest then obtainable, but this only slightly detracts from the excellent effect achieved by sound design and good proportion, both inside and out.

THE NEW WALK

The New Walk itself was laid out in 1785. The graceful iron lamp standards probably date from quite early in the nineteenth century and here and there, among later buildings, may be seen pretty Regency houses and stuccoed blocks that show both how cheerful and pleasing this covering can be when it is well and freshly painted and how ugly and dismal it looks when shabby and neglected.

THE MUSEUM

The portico and original front of the Museum are an imposing and on the whole successful essay in the Classical Grand (stucco) Manner. The building was originally the Proprietary School (Nonconformist) and was erected in 1837 from the designs of J. A. Hansom, the architect of the Birmingham Town Hall and the inventor of the Hansom Cab. The south wing is a less happy experiment in the use of honest (and economical) whitish-yellow brick. The north wing was built and most of the interior reconstructed in the present century. The Museum is open from 10 a.m. to 5.30 p.m. on weekdays and 2 p.m. to 5.30 p.m. on Sundays throughout the year.

KING STREET
REGENT ROAD
PRINCESS ROAD

These streets and the neighbouring streets and squares are interesting because they represent the planned development of a new residential area, corresponding to better-known contemporary developments in London but in the main actually built up rather later. The Crescent at the top of King Street was built about 1825 and Crescent Cottages opposite are dated 1836. The fine vista which the street provides was originally terminated by a classical building, Trinity Church, built in 1838. The Church is still there but its style became so unfashionable that the whole façade was rebuilt, very differently, in the second half of the century.

HUMBERSTONE GATE Amongst a muddle of later buildings Spa Place stands out as a planned block, a little earlier than the Crescent. (Miss Watts, in the second edition (1820) of *A Walk Through Leicester* speaks of 'a range of new and handsome buildings, called Spa-Place, from a chalybeate spring found there, which, though furnished by the proprietor with neat marble baths and every convenient appendage for bathing, has not been found sufficiently impregnated with mineral properties to bring it into use'.) The houses are now shabby, but the doorways are worth noting.

EARLY CHURCHES The building of Holy Cross Priory Church was begun in 1817 (that is to say, it was put up as soon as the building of Catholic churches was permitted by law, just as the Great Meeting was put up as soon as Nonconformist places of worship were allowed.) It was afterwards enlarged, but the original structure is, I think, still recognizable as the central part of what is now Blackfriars Hall. The first Anglican church to be built in Leicester after the Reformation was St. George's (about 1827). This building, which was in the Decorated style, was, however, almost completely destroyed by fire in the present century and I do not know how closely, if at all, the original lines were followed in its rebuilding.

THE SUBURBS At the end of the eighteenth and the beginning of the nineteenth century, trim villas and substantial houses were beginning to be built outside the town proper, mainly on the London and the Belgrave Road. A few of these survive, of which the best example is 'The Firs', Stoneygate: the carefully adapted front of the Masonic Hall preserves the character of a rather more urban type.

THE STUCCO PERIOD Important stuccoed buildings, other than those already mentioned, are Phoenix House in Welford Place (originally the offices of the Phoenix Assurance Co., later those of Stone & Co., and subsequently completely rebuilt in the 1970's, retaining the original façade), the Baptist Chapel (1830) in Charles Street and the 'Pork Pie' Chapel (1845) in Belvoir Street (now part of the City Adult Education Centre.) This last was an architectural joke for a century but is perhaps now old enough to be taken seriously.

THE CORN EXCHANGE This highly individual building takes us just beyond the half-century. The building, as we know it, is the creation of the gifted local architect, W. F. Ordish, who, soon after 1850, added the clock tower and the outside staircase to an existing structure. Severely criticized by the advocates of the newer styles, he maintained, sensibly and modestly, that 'he had done what he was required to do'.

116

In the late 1960's the Corn Exchange was extensively refurbished and restored, as part of the market redevelopment, and the stalls were set back to allow the building to be seen to advantage once more. The statue of the 5th Duke of Rutland, erected to commemorate his 50th Anniversary of service as Lord Lieutenant of Leicestershire, was returned to the site.

THE LATER NINETEENTH CENTURY

We are hardly yet aware of the difference between good and bad in the architecture of the later nineteenth century. It was a period in which people experimented in a bewildering variety of styles so that no stable tradition was established in which the ordinary run of architects could follow with success the lead given by the most gifted. It would, however, be a mistake to suppose that because almost all these styles are out of fashion now, they produced no good buildings. We shall be able to sort them out better in fifty years' time.

CHURCHES AND CHAPELS

During this period, the Gothic revival flowered and faded. It gave us a number of new churches in which medieval styles of architecture were followed with more or less success—St. John the Divine (1854), St. Andrew's (1862), St. Matthew's (1865), St. Paul's (1871), St. Mark's (1872), St. Leonard's—on a medieval site—(1876), St. Saviour's (1877), St. Peter's (about 1878). The well-intentioned use of local stone in many of them has hardly justified itself. Quarried granite, set in a close crazy pattern, produces a much harsher effect than Forest stone, used in the traditional way with a natural face outwards.

Most of the chapels were distinctly bashful about the use of Gothic styles, but Victoria Road Church (Baptist 1876), St. Andrew's Church, King Richard's Road (Methodist 1878) and St. Stephen's[1] (U.R.C.) adopted the form associated with Anglican churches and boldy raised spires to Heaven.

Of the old churches, St. Martin's was practically rebuilt externally and the others were heavily restored inside. The work was not done as we should wish to see it done now and the results are confusing and exasperating to archaeologists. It must be remembered, however, that the alternative to restoration was probably demolition and on the whole we have reason to be moderately grateful for the skill with which the Victorian architects

[1] 'The first St. Stephen's occupied a prominent site in London Road where the Wyvern Buildings now stand. It was opened in 1869 and was seated for about 800. Twenty-four years later, the site was sold for £10,000, and the church was taken down and rebuilt, with several architectural improvements, in its present position. The style of the new building was similar, but on a smaller scale'—*St. Stephen's Presbyterian Church of England, Leicester*, by Rev. George B. Burnet, M.A., 1932. (The Wyvern Buildings, since demolished, were just to the north of the station on London Road.)

performed their tasks and the sympathy with which they tried to follow the original intention.

Certainly, almost any restoration would have been preferable to the complete demolition of the old Wyggeston's Hospital and its chapel. (It was in one corner of the Alderman Newton's Boys' School playground, in St. Martins.) New hospital buildings, erected in the nineteenth century, were moderately convenient, though not of any great architectural merit, but they were on a fine and spacious site in Fosse Road South. These in their turn however have been demolished and the present hospital buildings with their new chapel, erected in 1968, stand on a small portion of the site the greater part of which has been given over to commercial development and houses.

FACTORIES AND OFFICES

Fortunately, Leicester architects did not follow the disciples of Ruskin very far in applying a purely ecclesiastical style to commercial buildings. The factories of H. T. H. Peck, by the West Bridge, and of Frisby and Jarvis (originally Thompson's) by the North Bridge, are straightforward, solid buildings with a monumental quality that is distinctly impressive. Some office buildings in Millstone Lane, the former Water Offices in Bowling Green Street (now the Juvenile Court) and the savings bank in St. Martin's are in what Spencer's Guide (1878) calls 'that adaptation of the Gothic style which has proved so convenient for public buildings generally'. But on the whole it seems to have been the exuberance of later styles that touched the imagination of Leicester architects and business men. Looking along Granby Street one can understand (though one may deprecate his adjective) what Ruskin meant when he spoke of 'the foul torrent of the Renaissance'.

THE TOWN HALL

It was, in all probability, a fortunate thing that in 1875 the City Fathers resisted the temptation to build a Gothic town hall. They were wise enough to select a central but quiet site, to choose a good architect, F. J. Hames, and to approve his plans for a quiet brick building in 'the style of the reign of Queen Anne'.[1] It is surely one of the best public buildings that the decade produced in any provincial English town.

DOMESTIC ARCHITECTURE

Whatever may be said against Victorian domestic architecture, there is this to be said in its favour: there was approximately enough of it. The middle classes (the aristocracy had gone from Leicester) were all comfortably housed; the working classes were all housed.

The other thing that is worth noticing here—discussion of the vast mass of surviving material would be impossible—is that some of it is very rapidly disappearing. The older type of workman's dwelling is already a museum

[1] I quote again from *Spencer's Handy Guide* (Supplement, 1878). The building is not in what we should now call Queen Anne style: the label does not matter much, but I should say that the building shows Flemish influence.

piece. At the Newarke Houses Museum, two rooms have been built up to show the home surroundings in which framework-knitting and bootmaking were carried on. It might almost have been worthwhile to consider preserving, as a whole, such a Dickensian nook as Stead's Place off Millstone Lane. But this has been completely swept away and I have no doubt that the former inhabitants are grateful for the much better modern houses to which they have moved.

At the other end of the scale, none of the really large houses are any longer private residences. Some have been pulled down, some shorn of their amenities of gardens and paddocks and converted to other uses. Brookfield, however, though its function has changed and changed again, still looks what it once was—a leading Victorian citizen's pleasant home.

OTHER BUILDINGS

When we have tired of the present fashion for severe straight lines, we shall look again, and with more favourable eyes, at many buildings whose real merits we now overlook because we dislike the colour of their material or because we consider their ornament 'fussy'. Without anticipating the verdict, it may be suggested that the Midland and National Westminster Banks on Granby Street (early in the period) and the Midland Station and the Grand Hotel (at the very end of it) have earned the right to come before a court of appeal. The National Westminster Bank, on St. Martin's, an unquestionably fine building, just belongs to the present century. I doubt if we shall ever find the Clock Tower (1868) more than useful and interesting but on these grounds alone it may make a good case for freedom to enjoy a long life.

FURTHER INFORMATION

Very little has been written in general description of eighteenth and nineteenth century buildings.

A Walk Through Leicester, by Miss S. Watts (second edition, 1820, 1st ed. reprinted by Leicester University Press, 1968) describes the town and its antiquities at that date. Guide-books of various dates describe the buildings that were then thought important or beautiful, in particular, *Spencer's Illustrated Handy Guide to Leicester* (my copy is the third edition, with a supplement bringing the information up to 1878) gives many useful descriptions, illustrations, and dates, besides delivering or quoting some illuminating contemporary criticisms. An earlier and shorter account is that of the Rev. O. Curtis, in *A Topographical History of the County of Leicester,* 1831. The notes by Mr. S. H. Skillington on the illustrations to *A Historical Guide to Leicester* (1933) may be regarded as authoritative and, for this period, the descriptions in *A Guide to Leicester and District* (1907), by Mrs. G. Clarke Nuttall, are trustworthy, as are also those in Mrs. Fielding Johnson's *Glimpses of Ancient Leicester* (second edition, 1906, with supplementary notes covering the period 1800-50).

The modern churches and some other buildings are described in the Building Record compiled during the war for N.F.S. purposes.

Section III

(a) DANIEL DEFOE[1]

(c. 1720)

[ONE of Defoe's most popular and valuable journalistic enterprises was a comprehensive survey of the England of his day. Unlike Leland, who was a single-minded antiquary, he wrote for the general public and was chiefly concerned to record the economic picture. This being the case, it is worth noticing that he gives only a few surprised lines to the manufacturing activities of Leicester, going on to describe at much greater length the livestock production of Leicestershire and the neighbouring counties.]

Leicester is an ancient large and populous town, containing about five parishes, 'tis the capital of the county of Leicester, and stands on the River Soar, which rises not far from that High Cross I mention'd before: They have a considerable manufacture carry'd on here, & in several of the market towns round for weaving stockings by frames; and one would scarce think it possible so small an article of trade could employ such multitudes of people as it does; for the whole county seems to be employ'd in it: as also Nottingham and Darby, of which hereafter.

Warwickshire and Northamptonshire are not so full of antiquities, large towns, and gentlemen's seats, but this county of Leicester is as empty. The whole county seems to be taken up in country business, such as the manufactures above, but particularly in breeding and feeding cattle; the largest sheep and horses in England are found here, and hence it comes to pass too, that they are in consequence a vast magazine of wool for the rest of the nation; even most of the gentlemen are grasiers, and in some places the grasiers are so rich, that they grow gentlemen: 'tis not an uncommon thing for grasiers here to rent farms from 500£ to two thousand pounds a year rent.

.   .   .   .   .

I should not pass over this just remark of the town, or as Mr. Cambden calls it, city of Leicester, namely that as it was formerly a very strong and well fortify'd town being situated to great advantage for strength, the river compassing it half about, so it was again fortify'd in the late unhappy wars, and being garrison'd by the Parliament forces, was assaulted by the Royalists, and being obstinately defended, was taken

---

[1] *A Tour Through England and Wales*
Divided into Circuits of Journies
by Daniel Defoe

Letter VII. Containing a description of part of Cheshire, Shropshire, Wales, Staffordshire, Warwickshire, Northamptonshire, Leicestershire, Lincolnshire, Rutlandshire, and Bedfordshire.

'THE FIRS', LONDON ROAD: THE DIGNITY OF THE CLASSICAL TRADITION BEFORE
THE EFFECT OF THE INDUSTRIAL REVOLUTION

HIGH STREET IN THE MID-1920s

LEICESTER IN 1828, BEFORE THE
FIRST INDUSTRIAL EXPANSION

DE MONTFORT HALL (1913)

HIGH LIVING IN LEICESTER
TOWER BLOCKS OF FLATS AT ROWLATTS HILL (1966)

sword in hand, with a great slaughter, and not without the loss also of several of the inhabitants, who too rashly concern'd themselves in opposing the conquerors. They preserve here a most remarkable piece of antiquity, being a piece of mosaick work at the bottom of a cellar; 'tis the story of Actæon, and his being kill'd by his own hounds, wrought as a pavement in a most exquisite manner; the stones are small, and of only two colours, white and brown, or chestnut, and very small.

The great Henry, Duke of Lancaster, and the earl his father lye both bury'd in this town, in the hospital church, without the south gate, which church and hospital also the said duke was the founder of; but there is no monument to be found that shews the particular place of their interment.

[From the appendix to this letter, strongly advocating the extension of the turnpike system.]

Suppose you take the other northern road namely, by St. Albans, Dunstable, Hockley, Newport Pagnell, Northampton, Leicester, and Nottingham or Darby: On this road, after you are pass'd Dunstable, which, as on the other way, is about 30 miles, you enter the deep clays, which are so surprisingly soft, that it is perfectly frightful to travellers, and it has been the wonder of foreigners, how, considering the great numbers of carriages which are continually passing with heavy loads, those ways have been made practicable; indeed the great number of horses every year kill'd by the excess of labour in those heavy ways, has been such a charge to the country, that new building of causeways, as the Romans did of old, seems to me to be a much easier expence: From Hockley to Northampton, thence to Harborough, and Leicester, and thence to the very bank of Trent these terrible clays continue; at Nottingham you are pass'd them, and the forest of Sherwood yields a hard and pleasant road for 30 miles together.

(b) CARL PHILIPP MORITZ[1]
(1782)

[Moritz visited England in the summer of 1782 and described his experiences in a series of letters to Friedrich Gedike, a well-known Prussian educationist. About half his book consists of a valuable and entertaining description of London; the remainder describes a journey via Oxford and Birmingham to the Peak of Derbyshire. He passed through Leicestershire on his way back to London.]

Towards evening I came to a pleasant meadow just before I got to Leicester, through which a foot-path led me to the town, which made a good appearance as I viewed it lengthways, & indeed much larger than it really is.

I went up a long street before I got to the house from which the post-coaches set out, & which is also an inn. I here learnt that the stage was to set out that evening for London, but that the inside was already full; some places were however still left on the outside.

Being obliged to bestir myself to get back to London, as the time drew near, when the Hambro' captain, with whom I intend to return, had fixed his departure, I determined to take a place as far as Northampton on the outside.

But this ride from Leicester to Northampton, I shall remember as long as I live.

The coach drove from the yard through a part of the house. The inside passengers got in, in the yard, but we on the outside were obliged to clamber up in the public street, because we should have had no room for our heads to pass under the gateway.

My companions on the top of the coach, were a farmer, a young man very decently dressed, & a black-a-moor.

The getting up alone was at the risk of one's life; and when I was up, I was obliged to sit just at the corner of the coach, with nothing to hold by, but a sort of little handle, fastened on the side. I sat nearest the

[1] TRAVELS
chiefly on foot
through
Several parts of England
in
1782
described
In Letters to a Friend

By Charles P. Moritz
A Literary Gentleman of Berlin
Translated from the German
By A Lady
London.
Printed for G. G. & J. Robinson, Pater-noster Row
1795.

wheel; & the moment that we set off, I fancied that I saw certain death await me. All I could do, was to take still faster hold of the handle, & to be more & more careful to preserve my balance.

The machine now rolled along with prodigious rapidity, over the stones through the town, & every moment we seemed to fly into the air; so that it was almost a miracle, that we still stuck to the coach, & did not fall off. We seemed to be thus on the wing, & to fly as often as we passed through a village, or went down an hill.

At last the being continually in fear of my life, became insupportable, & as we were going up a hill, & consequently proceeding rather slower than usual, I crept from the top of the coach, & got snug into the basket.

'O sir, sir, you will be shaken to death' said the black; but I flattered myself, he exaggerated the unpleasantness of my post.

As long as we went up hill, it was easy & pleasant. And having had little or no sleep the night before, I was almost asleep among the trunks & the packages; but how was the case altered when we came to go down hill; then all the trunks & parcels began, as it were, to dance around me and every thing in the basket seemed to be alive; & I every moment received from them such violent blows, that I thought my last hour was come. I now found that what the black had told me, was no exaggeration; but all my complaints were useless. I was obliged to suffer this torture nearly an hour, till we came to another hill again, when quite shaken to pieces & sadly bruised, I again crept to the top of the coach, & took possession of my former seat.

'Ah, did I not tell you, that you would be shaken to death?' said the black, as I was getting up, but I made him no reply. Indeed I was ashamed; and I now write this as a warning to all strangers to stage-coaches who may happen to take it into their heads, without being used to it, to take a place on the outside of an English post-coach; and still more, a place in the basket.

About midnight we arrived at Harborough.

(c) WILLIAM COBBETT[1]
(1830)

[Cobbett was, amongst many other things, a politician, but he played a lone hand amongst politicians. He was eccentric enough to think that the primary duty of statesmen was to see that the countryman was able to live a decent life under decent conditions. It was characteristic of his bias that he walked out from Leicester to Knighton and Aylestone to look for abuses which would move him to indignation: it is significant

[1] *Rural Rides* by William Cobbett. There have been many editions since the Rides were first published in the Political Register. The most complete and satisfactory is that edited by G. D. H. and Margaret Cole and published by Peter Davies in 1930.

that he found them there. Leicester would not have grown as it did if it had been only the town workers who suffered from bad housing and starvation wages.]

We got to Leicester on the 24th [of April], at about half-after five o'clock: and the time appointed for the lecture was six. Leicester is a very fine town; spacious streets, fine inns, fine shops, and containing, they say, thirty or forty thousand people. It is well stocked with jails, of which a new one, in addition to the rest, has just been built, covering three acres of ground! And, as if *proud* of it, the grand portal has little turrets in the castle style, with *embrasures* in miniature on the caps of the turrets. Nothing speaks the want of reflection in the people so much as the self-gratulation which they appear to feel in these edifices in their several towns. Instead of expressing shame at the indubitable proofs of the horrible increase of misery and crime, they really boast of these 'improvements' as they call them. Our forefathers built abbeys and priories and churches, and they made such use of them that jails were nearly unnecessary. We, their sons, have knocked down the abbeys and priories; suffered half the parsonage-houses and churches to pretty nearly tumble down, and make such uses of the remainder, that jails and tread-mills and dungeons have now become the most striking edifices in every county in the kingdom.

Yesterday morning (Sunday the 24th) I walked out to the village of Knighton, two miles on the Bosworth road, where I breakfasted, and then walked back. This morning I walked out to Hailstone, nearly three miles on the Lutterworth road, and got my breakfast there. You have nothing to do but walk through these villages, to see the cause of the increase of the jails. Standing on the hill at Knighton, you see the three ancient and lofty and beautiful spires rising up at Leicester; you see the river winding down through a broad bed of the most beautiful meadows that man ever set his eyes on; you see the bright verdure covering all the land, even to the tops of the hills, with here and there a little wood, as if made by God to give variety to the scene, for the river brings the coal in abundance, for fuel, and the earth gives the brick and the tile in abundance. But go down into the villages; invited by the spires rising up amongst the trees in the dells, at scarcely ever more than a mile or two apart; invited by those spires, go down into these villages, view the large, and once the most beautiful churches; see the parson's house, large, and in the midst of pleasure-gardens; and then look at the miserable sheds in which the labourers reside! Look at these hovels, made of mud and of straw; bits of glass, or of old off-cast windows, without frames or hinges, frequently, but merely stuck in the mud wall. Enter them, and look at the bits of chairs or stools; the wretched boards tacked together, to serve for a table; the floor of pebble, broken brick, or of the bare ground, look at the thing called a bed; and survey the rags on the backs of the wretched inhabitants; then wonder, if you can, that the jails and dungeons and treadmills increase, and that a standing army and barracks are become the favourite establishments of England!

(d) DR. JOHN BARCLAY[1]
(1864)

[Dr. Barclay gave two lectures to the Literary and Philosophical Society on Modern Leicester. The first, delivered in 1857, was severely critical: it is very briefly summarized in the Society's Transactions. The second, from which the following extracts are taken, was reprinted as a pamphlet which is in the Reference Library (Pamphlets, Vol. 83).]

It is surprising how even the general aspect of the town has changed since my last lecture. One spire, alas, that of St. Martin's, which represented the masculine strength and beauty, as contrasted with the more delicate feminine gracefulness of St. Mary's—has disappeared. On all sides vast blocks of warehouses have arisen, while the development of new manufactures, or the substitution of steam machinery for hand-labour has raised a forest of long factory chimneys. Twenty years and two months ago, when taking my first survey of the town, with the inhabitants of which I proposed to cast in my lot, I counted with difficulty 50 chimneys. There were, I believe, 59. Sergeant Wright calculates them now at nearly 250; and this increase of prosperity has not brought with it any drawback. Thanks to the judicious manner in which the Town Council have carried out the provisions of the Smoke Act . . . there is less smoke discharged from our 250 chimneys than formerly came from 50.

If visitors praise our atmosphere they execrate our streets. With the exception of the Market Place and one or two closely adjoining streets, the foot-pavement is only a shade better than it was seven years ago. True, the small flattened block of granite has been substituted in many places for the old kidney-shaped stone still to be found in too many localities, but at its best this is only what in London is considered fit for horses, and, I speak advisedly, a stranger will generally select the middle of the street as less trying to the feet of the pedestrian than the footway.

The vast system of drainage has I believe been almost completed, and will serve for the necessities of a greatly increased population. This and the ample supply of water have so far as can be judged from the limited time for experience and observation, exercised a marked influence on the health of the town, so that we now stand very high in place of very low in the health catalogue of the Registrar General. I fear the problem of the utilization of sewage is still unsolved. . . .

---

[1] *Modern Leicester*, Part II. A lecture delivered before the Leicester Literary and Philosophical Society, 22 February 1864, by John Barclay, M.D., F.R.C.P. Reprinted from the *Leicester Advertiser*, Leicester, printed by Wm. Penn Cox, Advertiser Office, Market Place.

Commencing now with the different approaches to the town; we find the London-road still our West End. The extension of gas beyond the second milestone has brought Stoneygate almost within the limits of the town itself—villas and handsome residences have risen up with amazing rapidity. . . . On both sides of the London-road have terraces and rows of houses been erected, none of which seem ever to be without a tenant for a day. To the westward of it we have De Montfort-square and streets, and the plans are already formed for the still further extension of building along the New Walk, and fronting the Occupation-road;[1] and no approach to the town can impress a stranger so much with the rapidly increasing wealth and prosperity of the community; and I may add that no part of the town testifies as plainly as this to the improved taste of our architects and designers. To the Eastward of the London-road again have numerous streets been laid out clustering round the grounds of the Collegiate School. A proposed street communicating between the London-road and the top of Sparkenhoe-street will vastly improve the accessibility of the latter. The difficulty of approach has probably caused most or all of the houses in this district to be of the second class only.

Beyond this again come new streets of the third-class houses, an entire new district. . . . In Humberstone-gate and Humberstone-road there are not many changes directly abutting on the throughfare. . . . The poor cricket ground, whose doom was just sealed when my last lecture was given has been entirely laid out in streets, and is already pretty well built over. Beyond that are miles of streets, what is called New Leicester—indeed a new town has risen up there, Brunswick-street, Curzon-street, Stanley-street, Cobden-street, running away into what, only a few years ago, were green fields and pastures.

Belgrave-gate has been much altered by the continuation of houses on the eastern side, from Britannia-street, right down to the Horse-water.

To the north, and in the direction of the Abbey, either from the tenure under which the property is held, or the lowness of the situation, the inhabitants do not seem so much inclined to extend their building propensities. Still we have some new houses in the course of erection just beyond the North Bridge. There are some most offensive dyeworks there which are of themselves quite enough to frighten anyone away from the neighbourhood.

Coming round to the Hinckley-road we find the most surprising changes. Danett's Hall is swept away, and new streets laid out on its site. . . . I cannot forbear the expression of a regret that the Danett's Hall estate was not secured as a place of recreation for the public—a People's Park. Fifty or a hundred years hence, if we go on increasing at our present rate, immense sums will probably have to be laid out to purchase breathing space for the inhabitants. We have now no cricket ground; . . .

[1] University Road.

126

I do not know if an idea that has occurred to me in examining this neighbourhood may be altogether chimerical. It would be to create an arboretum on that large waste space extending from the back of the castle to the extreme end of Braunstone-gate. . . .

Houses have also extended since my last lecture along the Aylestone-road, where building is still going on of second- and third-class houses.

With Knighton Hill we complete the circuit of the town. The Cemetery and the Asylum are likely to be a bar to much extension of building in this direction.

That the cattle market[1] is a horrible nuisance no one will, I think, deny, I am sure none will say a word in support of it who have to barricade their doors against the filthy accumulations that make the streets look and smell like a cow-shed for a couple of days. In my own part of the town we are quite blockaded, and a perilous passage can only be effected by a swift sailer on wheels, or a counterpart of an ironclad, impervious to the Greek fire of our beseigers. Surely some field on the close vicinity of the town could be devoted to this purpose, as it is in Edinburgh and Falkirk, and the great northern markets.

The widening of Cart's Lane—so called, I suppose, on the *lucus a non lucendo* principle, because two carts could not pass, is a most important improvement.

The new buildings of a commercial character are very numerous; . . . The improvement in this class of buildings is most marked. . . . Almost the first step towards improvement was in the shop and warehouses of Messrs. Swain & Latchmore (formerly Swain & Paddy) in Southgate-street.[2] The front is here decorated with coloured encaustic tiles let into the brickwork. I do not know that this is a style to be followed, but I mention it as a step in the right direction. . . .

Another very recently erected is the gas office in Millstone-lane. This is one of the most satisfactory buildings we have. It is a proof of how well the Gothic style may be adapted for such a building.

I think we may very surely hope that we shall go on from good to better. The spirit of enterprise, if unchecked by any commercial crisis, will lead to the continuance of the honourable rivalry that has already produced such good results. Undoubtedly the same objection will always hold good to Leicester as a whole that I mention as applying to buildings, that enlargements and alterations are invariably undesirable. But what is possible with an old building—to pull it down—is simply impossible with an old town—and Leicester must ever remain an enlarged country town. Irregularly laid out, and with no other plan than the highways to other towns, we can never hope to have such streets as we see in Edinburgh or even Glasgow, or Liverpool, or Manchester.

[1] The site of the old Cattle Market was on the site in which stands the New Town Hall'—*Spencer's Handy Guide* (1878).
[2] Actually in Highcross Street.

The best street we have is the miserable Sanvy-gate. Something may be made by & bye of Humberstone-gate. But we have several open spaces—the Market Place, the Hay Market, Welford Place, which such skill as has dealt with Paris might convert into fine Piazzas or irregular squares. The best we can hope for is that the taste of builders and architects may gradually produce some congruity out of the multifarious elements that now constitute our streets.

PART V

TWENTIETH CENTURY LEICESTER
by Jack Simmons

Section I

TWENTIETH CENTURY LEICESTER

THE growth of Leicester in the nineteenth century was spectacular. In 1901 the population was more than twelve times as large as it had been a hundred years before. No similar expansion has occurred since. In the following sixty years the number of people living within the borough boundary rose from 212,000 to 270,000. But such boundaries are artificial at any time; and in the twentieth century they have become more artificial still, when the quickening of transport has enabled people to live further and further from their work and in almost all British towns has encouraged the development of large suburbs, or even whole satellite towns, outside the limits of urban government. In these years a 'Greater Leicester' emerges, comprising the old town of Leicester, whose history lies at the heart of this book, its nineteenth-century extensions, and the further extensions that have now carried the area of continuous housing and urban development from Syston to Whetstone, from Kirby Muxloe to Thurnby. Thus defined, by 1971, Greater Leicester comprised some 500,000 people.

The main instruments of this great change have been first the electric tram, then the motor car and the motor bus. The Corporation bought out the private company that had operated the horse tramways in 1901, and the system was electrified in 1904-05. The Edwardian extension of the prosperous building of Stoneygate southwards along the London Road and into the parish of Oadby was an obvious consequence of the change. Motor cars made their way gradually—the whole country had fewer than 130,000 of them when the first World War broke out. But that war, among many other things, demonstrated their value, and when peace returned they multiplied fast. No more big houses were built, with ample gardens, in south-east Leicester; those who could afford to live like that now chose to move further out—to the edge of Charnwood Forest, for example—and to run into Leicester by car for work or shopping. The Corporation began to operate motor buses in 1924; but, like many other authorities, it adopted them rather hesitantly at first (one of the earliest bus routes was discontinued after three years, in favour of trams), and it did not go over to them decisively until the 1930s. The trams disappeared completely in 1947-49.

The great industrial development of the nineteenth century had transformed the old town of Leicester; leaving, indeed, the main lines of its medieval street-plan intact, together with most of its chief medieval buildings, but effacing almost everything else in favour of new industrial and commercial building. The process did not stop in 1900. The High

Street was widened—and robbed of all trace of its past—in 1902. In 1904 the entrance to the Newarke was opened up through the demolition of the old houses that had abutted on the Magazine Gateway. In May of that same year the ancient annual fair in the broad Humberstone Gate was held for the last time. As an obstruction to traffic, a useless survival from antiquity, it was swept away. But not everything was destruction in the cause of commercial progress. The town added to its social and cultural amenities too: with the very substantial premises opened by the Young Men's Christian Association (whose Leicester branch flourished, numbering 600 members), with the De Montfort Hall, which gave the town easily the finest large auditorium for concerts in the Midlands, in 1913.

Ever since the 1870s the town's economy had been increasingly diversified, with the growth of engineering side by side with the ancient hosiery industry and the more recently-established manufacture of boots and shoes. The tendency continued in the early years of the twentieth century, in the development of the making of scientific instruments and typewriters: not heavy engineering—Leicester has never had much of that—but light work, in which, as in the town's older industries, women were extensively employed as well as men.

Such was the town when war broke out in 1914: a prosperous place, comfortable for the majority of its people, maintaining its old radical tradition in politics (with Ramsay MacDonald as one of its Members of Parliament) and its old preference for nonconformity in religion. The war made no peculiar impact upon it; none that was markedly different from that on other inland towns in the country. No Zeppelin dropped bombs on Leicester (though ten people were killed in an air-raid at Loughborough, a dozen miles away, in 1916). The citizens played their part—responding slowly at first to the recruiting appeals of Kitchener and then, fired by the heroism of the 4th Leicester (Territorial) Battalion at the Hohenzollern Redoubt in October 1915, with eager generosity. Some £350,000 were subscribed to war charities in Leicester. As the fighting drew to its close a new appeal was launched, to commemorate the service of the men of the town and county. This was for funds to establish a University College: something that had long been talked of, both for its own sake and in order to enable Leicester to emulate its old rival Nottingham, which had had such a College of its own since 1881. The appeal succeeded, and with the help of the munificent gift of the old County Asylum building it enabled the new College to open its doors to students in October 1921.

At the end of the war the King conferred on Leicester the title of city, and in 1928 its chief magistrate became a Lord Mayor. At the same time the see of Leicester was revived, carved out of the diocese of Peterborough, and Dr. Cyril Bardsley became its first occupant in 1926.

These were all outward signs of Leicester's steadily increasing consequence. But they were mere formalities, no more: they could not affect her political power, her economic position, or her society. The depression that followed the end of the war hit her hard for a time; but many other towns in the country were hit harder. In the worst times of the early 1930s the number of the unemployed rose to over 16,000. Again, grave though this was, it represented a much smaller proportion than that in the great manufacturing towns of the North. Throughout these years Leicester kept a prosperity far above the average for the country as a whole: her characteristic kind of prosperity, expressed in high average earnings per family and a relatively low rate of unemployment, the income evenly diffused among the entire body of citizens.

The Corporation discharged many of its responsibilities well. In the years between the wars it built over 9,000 houses—to which must be added 3,000 more built by private enterprise with the aid of subsidies. Some of the municipal housing estates—notably that at Braunstone—could claim to be among the best of their time. The problems of the city's slums were tackled resolutely, above all in the district south of St. Margaret's church; and plans were formulated for much bigger clearances which, though they were held up by the second World War, have been implemented since. One major road development was undertaken, to relieve the intolerable congestion of the streets approaching the Clock Tower. This was Charles Street, which was completed in 1931. For the rest, however, it must be said that Leicester did no better in road-building than its fellows in these years. A bold plan of reconstruction was rejected by a town's poll in 1924, and though another was adopted in 1938 it had made little progress when the war broke out. Plans for a ring road to girdle the city—for the most part beyond its boundaries—were adopted in 1922; but argument with other local authorities delayed its construction. It is still a talking-point today.

All in all the Leicester of these years—the town depicted in C. P. Snow's novel *Time of Hope*—is an uninspiring place: not unpleasant or wholly unprogressive, but clearly lacking the raw vitality that in the nineteenth century had made it what it was, and showing nowhere much sign of leadership or true distinction.

The second World War made a more obviously important impact on Leicester than the first. Not that the city suffered much damage from air-raids. A few scattered bombs were dropped on it in 1940-41, doing some damage and killing a number of people; but Leicester was never the target of a major concentrated attack. The change appeared rather in social terms, arising from the forces that the war released. Higher education supplies a good example. In all its branches the city moved rapidly ahead: with the establishment of its Teachers' Training College (later renamed the College of Education and most agreeably housed at Scraptoft); the growth of the Colleges of Art and Technology, which later formed the City of Leicester Polytechnic, and the Charles Keene

133

College of Further Education; the equally striking growth of the University. The University College opened in 1921 had moved ahead very slowly at first, hampered by lack of funds; but with the great expansion of university education determined on at the close of the war it began to receive large-scale assistance from the Government and it leapt ahead, from 200 students in 1946 to 800 in 1957, when it was granted its charter as an independent University, to 3,750 in 1975.

This expansion has its monument, in the buildings entailed by it, and especially the group—mainly housing the science departments—erected in the 1960s, not least because of the quiet and respectful demeanour it displays towards a monument of an earlier age: Lutyens's noble Memorial, built in Victoria Park in 1926 to commemorate the dead in the first World War. A generation later the style of that monument, the very thinking that lay behind it, had fallen out of fashion. 'Brutalism' had come by then to be accounted an architectural virtue. All the more honour to Sir Leslie Martin and the City Planning Department, who agreed to restrict the height of the buildings adjacent to the memorial, leaving it still to accent the southern skyline, according to Lutyens's original intention.

Another sign of progress, no less characteristic of these years, was the series of large municipal housing schemes. The most striking of them was the pair of tall blocks at Rowlatt's Hill; the most important the St. Matthew's development, which restored life to a large tract of the city, between Humberstone Gate and Belgrave Gate, that had become a dreary, festering slum. Here, for the first time on a big scale, was a determined effort to reverse the trend of the past century and a half, for the citizens to move out of the centre of Leicester to new suburbs. It was a hopeful effort to arrest, before it was too late, the decay of the older quarters that has overtaken so many towns in the middle of the twentieth century, notably in the United States.

Reconstruction of the central area has been accomplished by large-scale replanning of the roads, a notable feature of which was the creation of the Southgates underpass, a scheme which entailed the greatest physical upheaval in the old town of Leicester since the Great Central Railway was driven across its western edge in the 1890s. In 1967-68 it gradually fell into place—though to the Leicester people watching it, and suffering daily from the discomforts it caused, the process seemed interminably slow. It brought some uncovenanted benefits, besides the improvements of the roads themselves and the liberation of the traffic passing over them. The building that had housed Vaughan College, for example, since 1908 stood in the path of the chief new road and had to be demolished. By a happy inspiration it was replaced by one that served a double purpose, providing on its upper floor a new Vaughan College, for the University's Department of Adult Education, and, below, an archaeological museum, admirably sited so as to face the Jewry Wall and to frame the foundations of the Roman bath building that had been exposed by excavation in 1936-39. In the years of reconstruction after the second World War, many historic towns in Europe were faced with comparable problems, of reconciling the imaginative treatment of their antiquities with the demands of modern traffic, housing, and administration. The Jewry Wall development in Leicester, though small and not beyond criticism, was a neat and intelligent solution to the problem, which attracted—and deserved—the attention of visitors from other parts of Britain and from overseas.

The Jewry Wall stands on the north side of what is now called St. Nicholas Circle, a large new road system with an hotel (built by an American company) at its centre. This one development alone has effaced a whole tract of the medieval town, and its ancient street plan, still easily visible in 1960, has now been almost entirely obliterated. The Castle stands unchanged here, however, with two of the medieval churches; and then to the south another new development has emerged, with the great extension of the Polytechnic (which incorporates the former College of Technology) and of the Royal Infirmary beyond it. The Infirmary extension is closely related to the inauguration of a medical school at the University, which took its first students in 1975.

These years, then, brought with them some clear and striking examples of what the Victorians called 'town improvement'. In some fields loss and gain were balanced. The city had already lost its one morning newspaper in 1921; in 1963 its two evening papers were reduced to one. On the other hand, Leicester was the first town in Britain to have its own local broadcasting station, opened—through a partnership between the B.B.C. and the City Council—in 1967. Meanwhile, the three old professional theatres had disappeared, leaving at one time nothing but the Little Theatre, where a valiant and successful company of amateurs kept the drama alive. Then, in 1963, the Phoenix rose from their ashes. That was a small theatre, but it provided excellent value for the money spent on it. In 1973 a new one, the Haymarket, much larger and more elaborately equipped, was opened; built into a substantial new shopping centre, immediately adjoining the Clock Tower. Most towns of Leicester's size have gone in for centres of this sort; very few have been able to place theirs so close to the heart of the old town. It is a walk of no more than three minutes from the Haymarket Centre to the Market Place, which still carries on its traditional business as it has done for 700 years.

The city has not been notable for many bold experiments. But then, if it had been, it would have been false to much of its own history. It has seldom, in the past, been a pioneer. Rather, it has concentrated on the cautious and shrewd improvement of existing patterns and techniques. In the nineteenth century Leicester's hosiery and footwear came to be widely exported; and it was the cradle of the European tourist industry.

In the twentieth century these products have been joined by others—electric clocks and lifts, for example, and optical lenses—that have carried the name of the city across the world. And yet, even in our rapidly-changing times, it has not been false to its ancient motto *Semper Eadem*. It is 'always the same' as it has been for centuries past: a market town and a local capital, on to which a great industrial development has been grafted.

FURTHER INFORMATION

Not much has yet been written on twentieth-century Leicester from a strictly historical point of view. By far the most important contribution has been made in the fourth volume of the *Victoria History of the County of Leicester* (1958), which is devoted exclusively to the city and includes a very clear account of its political, social and economic history down to 1955. See also R. G. Waddington, *Leicester: the Making of a Modern City* (1931), and for the first World War F. P. Armitage, *Leicester 1914-1918* (1933). One of the city's chief industries is discussed in A. G. Pool and G. Llewellyn, *The British Hosiery Industry: a Study in Competition* (3 parts, 1955-58). The history of the University College down to its incorporation as an independent university is dealt with in J. Simmons, *New University* (1958). Two planning reports are of special interest: the *Report* of the Leicestershire Regional Town Planning Joint Advisory Committee (1932) and W. K. Smigielski, *Leicester Traffic Plan* (1964).

On the buildings of the twentieth century see N. Pevsner, *The Buildings of England: Leicestershire and Rutland* (1960), and J. Simmons, *The City of Leicester* (3rd ed., 1960).

The most recent general account of the city's history is J. Simmons, *Leicester Past and Present* (2 vols., 1974). See also *Leicester and its Region*, ed. N. Pye (1972).

DATES FOR REFERENCE

General History		*Leicester*	
1902	Boer War ended	1902	High Street reconstructed
		1904	Electric trams inaugurated
1906	General election: return of Liberal Govt.		
1911	Parliament Act passed		
1914	Outbreak of first World War		
1918	First World War ends		
		1919	Title of 'city' conferred on Leicester
		1921	University College opened
1926	General Strike	1926	See of Leicester restored
1931	Formation of National Govt.	1931	New Charles Street completed
		1935	Extension of boundaries
1939	Outbreak of second World War		
1945	Second World War ends		

General History

Leicester

1949	Trams abolished
1957	University College becomes University of Leicester
1959	River Dove Water Scheme inaugurated
1967	Extension of boundaries
1974	County Borough of Leicester becomes a non-metropolitan district council forming part of new County.

Section II

TWENTIETH CENTURY BUILDINGS

NATIONAL WESTMINSTER BANK, ST. MARTIN'S

Built for a local bank, Pares', by a Leicester architect of fine taste, S. Perkins Pick. Imposing façade with two round turrets at the corners; handsome side elevation on to Grey Friars.

ALL SOULS CHURCH, AYLESTONE RD.

One of the last works of the distinguished Victorian architect G. F. Bodley (1907). The exterior is unimpressive, but inside the church has an unforgettable cool charm, achieved with economy and restraint. There is a window by Sir Ninian Comper in the north aisle.

DE MONTFORT HALL

Designed by Stockdale Harrison & Sons and built in 1913. A very large concert hall, seating 2,960 people; spacious, and well designed as a musical auditorium. It includes a good organ.

WAR MEMORIAL, VICTORIA PARK

By Sir Edwin Lutyens (1926). A tall arch, in Portland stone, pierced on four sides and crowned with a low dome. A smaller version of Lutyens's war memorial in Delhi. The two approaches from the east (London Rd.) and the north (University Rd.) are guarded by handsome wrought-iron gates. Two charming little pavilions flank the entrance from London Rd.

ST. BARNABAS BRANCH LIBRARY; SOUTHFIELDS BRANCH LIBRARY

By Symington, Prince & Pike (1937 and 1939 respectively). Two very similar brick buildings with drum towers whose windows light the main central space. They reflect the influence of Holden's celebrated London Transport stations.

ENGINEERING BUILDING, THE UNIVERSITY

By Stirling & Gowan (1963). Ten-storey glass tower with lecture-theatres and laboratories and top-lighted workshops below. A famous monument, widely acclaimed by architects and critics, in America as well as in this country, as one of the most important buildings to be erected in Britain in the 1960s.

FLETCHER BUILDING THE POLYTECHNIC

By the then Leicester City Architect, Stephen George (1965). A tall tower presiding over a range of two-storey buildings, displacing a large area of dilapidated houses and transforming a whole neighbourhood close to the centre of the city.

Section III

(a) THE END OF THE FIRST WORLD WAR, 11 NOVEMBER 1918[1]

IT was 2 o'clock: a sea of upturned faces surrounded an improvised platform in the Town Hall Square. The Mayor, Councillor Walter Lovell, was speaking,—'People of Leicester. The end of the terrible struggle has arrived. The enemy has acknowledged defeat. Four years' unexampled bravery of our sons, supported by the fortitude of the people at home, has met its reward, and at last we find ourselves in the victorious position of being able to dictate terms to the enemy'.

Calling on Alderman North to speak, the Mayor said that from the bottom of his heart he wished that this consummation had been Alderman North's portion, and that he had been able to announce to them that at last the enemy was vanquished.[2]

Alderman North was received with vociferous cheers.—'I hope all the people of Leicester will try to make themselves worthy of that liberty which has been preserved to us by the heroic efforts of our brave sons, who have for so long stood between us and the enemy of mankind—let your rejoicing be characterised by a sober and reasonable demeanour, such as becomes the gravity of the situation even as it is now. I hope you will not look upon the task as over and forget what has been done by our brave fellows. No sacrifice is too great for us at home by which we can show our gratitude to the men who have won the victory'.

Lieutenant Commander Pearse appealed to the public to be as brave in peace as in war, that there might be built up a prouder and a nobler England than they ever had before.

The Bishop of Peterborough hoped that the last shot had been fired and the last war finished; that this was the day when the new age would dawn upon Europe and upon the world, and that never again would the Nations go to war with one another, and that henceforth there would be among them fellowship, justice and peace.

(b) J. B. PRIESTLEY

[J. B. Priestley visits Leicester in the course of a tour of England.][3]

The sun had not set when I came into Leicester itself, which looked bright and new. In his *Guide to England,* Mr. Muirhead, in his comfortable fashion, calls it 'a busy and cheerful industrial place, for the most

[1] From F. P. Armitage, *Leicester 1914-1918* (1933), pp. 301-2.

[2] Alderman (Sir) Jonathan North had served as Mayor of Leicester for four years in succession (1914-18).

[3] From J. B. Priestley, *English Journey* (1934), pp. 118-127.

138

ENGINEERING BUILDING, UNIVERSITY OF LEICESTER

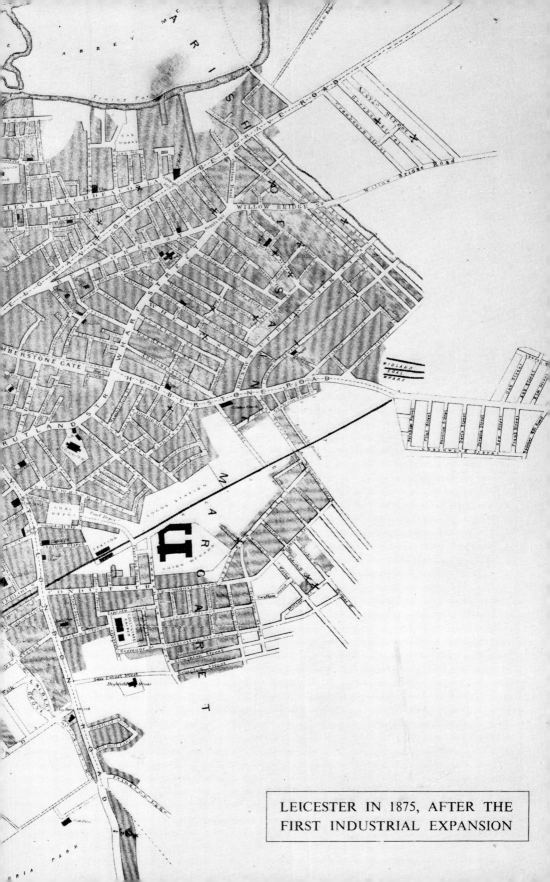

LEICESTER IN 1875, AFTER THE
FIRST INDUSTRIAL EXPANSION

HAYMARKET THEATRE : INTERIOR

part built of red brick', and for some hours after I had arrived there I found it impossible to improve upon that description and difficult even to amplify it. The citizens, who are proud of the place, boast that it is one of the cleanest manufacturing towns in this country, and they are quite right: it is. They also boast that it has a very enterprising town council, and I have no doubt it has. (Notice the Fire Station.) It is comparatively prosperous. You feel almost at once that it is a very worthy borough that is deservedly getting on in the world. But it is hard to believe that anything much has ever happened there. Actually it is very old and offers you a very rum mixed list of historical associations: for example, King Lear and his daughters lived here, if they ever lived anywhere; it is Simon de Montfort's town; the broken Cardinal Wolsey came here to die, and has now acquired a new immortality by having his name stamped on thousands of bales of stockings and underclothes; John Bunyan saw the siege here during the Civil War; and among its nineteenth-century citizens was the original Thomas Cook, who ran his first little excursion out of Leicester station. But somehow you do not believe in all these goings on. The town seems to have no atmosphere of its own. I felt I was quite ready to praise it, but was glad to think I did not live in it. There are many worse places I would rather live in. It seems to me to lack character, to be busy and cheerful and industrial and built of red brick, and to be nothing else. Such was my immediate impression. . . .

During dinner I examined the two local papers to see how I could spend my evening. A Leicester man had boasted to me that the town was now the chief sporting centre of the provinces, being able to offer you good examples of every sport, and notably boxing; but on this particular evening it had no sport to offer. So I asked the waiter, who was a Leicester lad born and bred, but who had somehow contrived to give himself a foreign look (he will probably go far, that boy) where I could go to see Leicester enjoying itself of an evening, and he suggested a certain dance-hall, which was having one of its 'popular nights'. So there I went, paying one and sixpence to go in and threepence to leave my hat and overcoat in the cloak-room. The hall itself, which had a balcony all round it, a large floor and a lighting equipment superior to that of most of the London hotels and supper-dancing places, was quite good; it could have comfortably entertained six times as many dancers as were there. Most of the patrons were young and there were nearly as many boys there as girls. They seemed to me to dance very well—fox-trots, quick-steps, rumbas, waltzes—and in a much more reserved and digni-fied fashion than their social superiors in the West End. They were, I imagine, mostly factory hands, and apart from an occasional guffawing from a group of lads, they were quiet and serious, as sedately intent on their steps as a conference of dancing teachers. I felt an intruder, and left after a quarter of an hour or so, only to discover that the music hall where I had formerly seen a good robust show was now given up to Constance Bennett. In the whole of Leicester that night, there was only one performance being given by living players, in a touring musical comedy. In a town with nearly a quarter of a million people, not without intelligence or money, this is not good enough. . . .

It was one of the directors of [the Imperial Typewriter Company] . . . who entertained me to lunch. He has a house in what seemed to me a very pleasant residential quarter of the town, a quarter with wide streets and detached villas. This particular house was of an excellent design, and when I was told that it had been built forty years before, when houses were rarely designed or executed with any taste, I was curious to learn why my host should have been so fortunate. It seems that Leicester has had for some time, more than forty years, a few citizens who have been first-class designers and craftsmen, and this house had been the creation of one of them. I remembered then that I had heard of these Leicester craftsmen before, and indeed knew one or two good artists who had come from this place.

(c) W. G. HOSKINS[1]

Perhaps it is the city of Leicester of which the exile can say: This is the corner of the world above all others that has a smile for me. Solid, Victorian, brick-built and prosaic, Leicester has none of the dramatic quality of Nottingham with its great castle rock dominating the city, none of the character of the blackened-stone towns of the industrial North. It has no real centre, least of all—praise God—a civic centre in councillor's concrete. It has no street of any real distinction. No stranger would ever get excited about it. But it has a small town homeliness (for all its three hundred thousand people), a comfortable feeling of Sunday dinners and security, of chapels and libraries and much earnest winter reading and lecturing, of life still revolving around 'the old clock Tower' as it did in grandfather's time, that many of us find appealing and satisfying in a world that is increasingly buried in soulless concrete: a delightful Betjeman town that one would not willingly see too much changed.

[1] From **W. G. Hoskins**, *Leicestershire: an illustrated Essay on the History of the Landscape* (1957), p. 133.

140

INDEX

Abbey of St. Mary de Pratis 39, 41, 46, 50, 53, 55, 68, 72, 78, 82, 84
—— site 53, 79, 86, 105, 126
—— Park 53, 106, 110
Abbot of St. Mary's 53, 58, 59, 60
Ad Pontem 25
Æthelflæd 29, 33
Aganippus, King 23
Agincourt 48
Agricola, Cnaeus Julius 23
Agriculture 5, 31, 44, 45, 65, 66, 86, 88, 93, 99, 120
Alfred, King 25, 29, 33
All Saints' (All Hallows) Church 37, 39, 41, 52, 59, 113
All Souls' Church 137
Ancaster 13
Andrews, C. Bruyn 98n
Angel Inn 37, 73
Anglia, East 28, 30, 66
Angles, 26, 27
—— Middle 27, 29, 32
Anstey 96n
Antoninus, Emperor 22, 24
Antoninus, Itinerary of (Antonine Itinerary) 24
Apple Gate, 36, 54
Apprenticeship 71, 95; pauper 95
Archaeological Journal 21, 81
Archaeological Society, Leicestershire 22, 34, 49, 55, 77, 80.
Architects, Leicester Society of 55, 81
Arden, Forest of 27, 57
Armada 69, 78
Armitage, F. P. 136, 138n
Arms, City 43
Art Gallery 105, 111
Ashby-de-la-Zouch 67, 72, 86
Assembly Rooms—see County Rooms
Asteley, Sir Bernard 85
Asylums 115, 127, 132
Augustine, St. 26, 32, 53.
Avon River (Warwickshire) 26
Aylestone (Hailstone) 52, 112, 123, 124
—— Road 43n, 127, 137.

Bakehouse Lane 36, 54
Bailiff, High 43
Bankers 96
Bank, Midland 113, 119
—— National Westminster (formerly National Provincial or Westminster, Pares', Parr's) 107, 113, 119, 137
—— Savings 118
Banks, Mr. 98
Baptists 101
Barclay, Dr. John 125
Bard, Colonel 85
Bardsley, Dr. C. 132
Barne Park 84

'Barrow Butchery' 99, 110
Basilica, 14, 16, 21, 22
Bateson, Miss E. M. 49, 55, 57n, 77
Bath, Roman 15, 16, 19, 22, 24, 135
Beauchamp, Isabel 82
Beaumanor 70, 84
Beaumont, de 40, 43
Beaumont Leys (Bellemontes Lease) 84, 105
Bede, Venerable 25, 32
Bedford 29
Belgae 13
Belgrave 111
Belgrave Gate (Rd.) 106, 108, 116, 126, 134
—— Hall, 112
—— House 112
Belgrave, Mr. 67
Belvoir 72
—— Street 116
Benfield, Dr., house 113, 114
Bent's Charity 96
Billson, C. J. 49, 55, 77, 81, 96n
Birmingham 107n, 122
—— Town Hall 115
Bishop's Water 83
Bishop Street Chapel 113, 114
Bishopric of Leicester 28, 29, 32, 39, 68, 132, 136
Black Death 5, 45, 46, 50
Black Friars 17, 36, 50, 55, 82
Blackfriars Hall 116
—— Street 55
Bladud, King 23
Blanchesmains, Robert 39, 50
Blank, E., 22
Blue Boar Lane 14, 16, 17, 22, 55, 98
—— Inn 37, 48, 51, 55
Blunt (tomb) 83
Boadicea 23
Bodley, G. F. 137
Bond Street 54, 97, 112
Boot manufacture 103, 119, 135
Borough English 44, 50
Boroughs, Five 29, 31
Bossu, Robert le 39n, 50, 51, 53, 82
Boston 59
Bosworth Field 48, 55, 66, 88
Boucher, Mr. 83
Bow Bridge 37, 48, 88
Bowdon, Lt-Colonel W. Butler 6, 58
Bowling Green Street 118
Bradgate 69, 72, 84
Braunstone 112, 133
—— Gate 106n, 127
Breedon 26
Bricks, use of 76, 84, 89, 97, 111
Britannia Street 126
Brokesby (tomb) 83
Brookfield 119

141

Trade Unions 109
Trajan, Emperor 22
Trams, electric 131, 136, 137
Trams, horse 107, 110, 131
Trent, River 13, 27, 88, 121
Trevelyan, G. M. 5, 43, 48, 70*n*
Trial by Battle 56
—— Jury 31, 56
—— Ordeal 56
Trinity, Holy, Church 116
Trintiy Hospital 41*n*, 49, 52, 55, 87, 88, 96, 97*n*, 113
Tripontium 25
Tusser, Thomas 45*n*

Unitarians 101
University 7, 115, 132, 134, 135, 136, 137
——Road 126*n*, 137
Uppingham 87, 89*n*

Vaughan family: Vaughan College, 102, 134
Venonae 25
Verulamium 25
Verometum, Vernemetum 25
Vespasian, Emperor 13, 23
Victoria County History, Leicestershire 34, 136
    Northamptonshire 25
—— Parade 96
—— Park 40, 106, 134, 137
——, Queen 110, 111
Victoria Road Church 117
Victorians 103

Wacher, J. S. 21, 22
Waddington, R. G. 136
Wages 99
Wales 23
Wall, Jewry—*see* Jewry Wall
——, Abbot Penny's 53, 76*n*, 84
Walls, Town 12, 18, 22, 29, 36, 53, 73, 82
Walpole, Horace 114
Wansford 88, 89*n*
War Memorial 134, 137
Warwick 72, 93
Warwickshire 27, 88, 120
Wash, the 26, 27
Water Offices 118
—— supplies and works 16, 74, 89, 96, 105, 109, 110, 125, 137
Watling Street 28, 30

Watts, Miss S. 116, 119
——, William 97
Webb, Beatrice and Sidney 107*n*
Welford Place 116, 128
Welland River 26, 29
Wesley, John 101
Wessex, West Saxons 25, 26, 29, 33
West Bridge 13, 18, 37, 54, 55, 83, 106*n*, 118
—— Field 30
Westcotes 106
Westminster Bank—*see* Bank, National Westminster
Whatton, John 66
Whetstone 131
Whetstone, Mr. 99
Whilton Lodge 25
White, Sir Thomas 71, 96
White Horse Inn 89*n*
Wigston, Roger—*see* Wygston, Roger
——, William—*see* Wyggeston, William
Wilfrid, St. 27, 32
William I 30, 49
—— III 30
Willoughby on the Wolds 25
Wilshere, J. 77
Winchester 29
—— Cardinal of 83
Winstanley, Charles 98
Wolsey, Cardinal 53, 68, 77, 87, 139
Wood Gate 54
Wool Combers 94
—— Trade 45, 46, 47, 48, 66, 94, 120
Workhouses 97, 105, 115
Wright, Sergeant 125
Wreake (Reeke) River 88
Wycliffe, John 46
Wyggeston, Roger—*see* Wygston, Roger
Wyggeston, William, 52, 66, 67, 72, 79, 80, 82
—— Boys School 110
——'s Hospital 37, 41*n*, 66, 76, 77, 82, 88, 96, 118
Wygston, Roger 79
Wygston, William—*see* Wyggeston, William
Wygston's House, Roger 37, 79, 81, 113, 114
Wyvern badge 43
—— Buildings 117*n*

Y.M.C.A. 132
Yeomanry, Leicestershire 103
York 25, 38